How To Be Appealing To Successful

BLACK MEN...
FOR BLACK WOMEN

By: Matthew C. Horne

Lightning Fast Book Publishing, LLC

P.O. Box 441328

Fort Washington, MD 20744

www.lfbookpublishing.com

All rights reserved. No part of this book may be reproduced or transmitted in any form or by any means—electronic, mechanical, photocopying, recording, or otherwise—without the written permission from the author, except for the inclusion of brief quotations in a review.

The author of this book provides strategies for appealing to high caliber successful black men. The literary offering provided is non-fictional and derived from the experiences and knowledge of the author. In the event that you use or implement any of the material in this book, the author and publisher assume no responsibility for your actions.

Copyright © 2020

Matthew C. Horne.

All rights reserved.

ISBN: 978-1-7348113-1-5

Table of Contents

Dedication	5
Preface	7
Chapter 1: What Is A Successful Black Man	11
Chapter 2: Find A Sound Minded Woman Mentor	27
Chapter 3: Consider The Source	39
Chapter 4: Don't Make Him Work For It	47
Chapter 5: He Has To Have More Than Me	59
Chapter 6: Size Him Up Accurately	71
Chapter 7: Be His peace	83
Chapter 8: Keep It Tight	95
Chapter 9: Despise Opportunistic Behavior	103
Chapter 10: It's Too Good To Be True	119
Chapter 11: The Defense Rests	133
Chapter 12: The Power To Change	149
Chapter 13: Love Is Not Enough	159
Chapter 14: It's Easy To Get Married	173
Chapter 15: It Means Nothing To Him	181
Chapter 16: Decided Advantages	193
Chapter 17: Calibrate Yourself	209
Chapter 18 : Emotional Availability	223
Bonus Chapter : Attraction	235

Dedication

This book is dedicated to all of the beautiful black women who desire healthy and lasting relationships with black men. As long as you continue to show up as the best version of yourself, the right man will recognize and cherish you.

You are undeniably the most beautiful creature that graces the planet.

Preface

With the amount of black women who are projected to not get married existing in epidemic proportion, I felt the need to contribute a thought provoking ideology to the black woman that could increase her chances of partnering with the black man she deems as ideal. This book is written to reset the norms amongst black men and women to a healthy place, and to facilitate a more progressive and enjoyable experience between black men and women.

Our consciousness is largely based on what we are exposed to and the story about ourselves that we accept. There are successful, loving, emotionally available, ambitious, and progressive black men who do exist, and desire to partner with black women. The myth of successful black men largely dating outside of their race is a fallacy. In my research, I found that the more successful the black man is, the more likely he is to marry a black woman.

If you arrive in the space of the successful black man postured to him, healed, emotionally mature, and intelligent, he will understand that you two are compatible and aligned. Choosing you will be an effortless decision.

My hope is that every black woman who reads this work will become calibrated to the high value black man that she desires and be positioned to experience a healthy and fulfilling life with a successful black man. My desire is that every norm that the matrix imposes on us concerning marriage rates and unhealthy relationship dynamics that exist in the black community are dispelled. I also desire for the perspective of the successful black man, concerning black women, to be understood and internalized, better equipping you for a lasting union with the successful black man.

If you show up as an evolved and centered version of yourself in life, it translates to more desirable and elevated experiences. If you bring this version of yourself to the high-value successful black men, you will experience the ideal man you desire, and be poised to be his final dating destination.

Chapter 1

What is a Successful Black Man

In a conversation with two black women, close to their fifties in age, this definition came into frame. Their displeasure with black men was that they were not ambitious, but lazy underachievers who wanted nothing substantial for themselves in life. This is the polar opposite of the man I am describing in this book. The successful black man is the man who possesses a vision beyond where he is no matter how successful he is, leaving him in a constant state of upward trajectory. He is the man who is actually who he says he is, never feeling the need to over inflate himself. He is humble—never feeling the need to wear his accomplishments on his sleeve, while, in the same breath, is fully aware of his place in the food chain based on the shortage of this type of black man in society. He is self-sufficient and can only be offered companionship from a woman. He treats everyone, including women, with respect. He's not full of himself, even though possessing these traits places him in rare air. He sees others as equals, not weighing a person's perceived value according to the world's standards of success. He's hardworking and dedicated to whatever his professional craft is. He's reliable and a solid rock for those he loves. He has a strong spiritual foundation and acknowledges God as his source of all. He doesn't wait for things to happen; he simply creates the situations he'd like to experience. He understands his God-given gifts make him self-sufficient, not solely lending his livelihood to a system that was not designed for him to win. He is a protector and a provider. He is a reliable presence in the life of his woman and those around him.

He Is A Visionary

This is one of the core essentials that make him as successful black man: no matter if he's still finding his way in life, or he's arrived at the pinnacles of success, he always has a vision beyond where he is, and is actively taking daily steps toward the fulfillment of that vision. He's perpetually flourishing because he has vision and doesn't park on whatever level he currently resides. Lots of men are all about lip service pertaining to what they're "going" to do or "about" to do. The successful black man is perpetually about action and in no way entrenched in lip service. He is solid in his core and removes himself from the presence of pretenders because he's attained success in a way that is contrary to how the unsuccessful man falsely perpetuates to anyone who will listen.

He has intelligence with his vision, so even if he suffers a setback, he's buffered himself mentally and financially for these occurrences, and is back in the game shortly due to his cerebral and tenacious approach to getting ahead and staying ahead in life.

You Can Stand Behind Him

You can safely support and stand behind him because when you two entered each other's lives, he already had a strain of tangible results that resulted from his ability to create and execute the various ambitions for his life that have propelled him forward. There's no pretenses with this man, only substance. It's difficult for a woman to submit to and stand behind a man who cannot create and execute a vision for his life. This is understandable, given you are biologically wired to seek protection and security on many levels from a man. His words are not a necessity concerning his plans both current and future; given his actions speak at a volume anyone can interpret without him saying a word.

He Has An Upward Trajectory

Given that he has proven, over time that he can create and execute a vision, he will always have an upward trajectory relating to success. Upward trajectory must be observed in the black man. There is a structure that thrives by the eradication of black men as a whole, coupled with the slower progression of black men. As a black woman, many times you will have figured some things out in terms of career and long-term financial wellbeing that some black men you have encountered may have not.

What must be observed is this man's upward trajectory. Even if he has not put things together as you have in life, his vision, drive, focus, and longevity in his vision must be taken into account. When you meet him, he will have results that solidify his ability to produce results. But, given the imbalance of successful black women to successful black men, you must take his trajectory into account.

Taking his trajectory into account does not mean you are settling if society does not perceive him to be on your level. It means that you intelligently understand the dating pool and are moving accordingly to bolster your chances of landing a solid mate.

If the man sits around and plays PlayStation all day and has zero ambition to move forward in life, you have every right to overlook him because he is not accepting his basic responsibilities in life as a man. If the man is making strides in his life and catapulting himself toward his vision, and you are actually into him, be patient. Trust the results that he has accumulated and understand that his upward trajectory will play out in a favorable way over time.

He is a Go-Getter

The successful black man is not waiting on life to happen to him. He is consistently and intentionally imposing his will on life.

This also creates a safety net of trust knowing that your man is ready to weather any storm you two may encounter in life's unpredictable weather. The go-getter approach commonly leads to a surplus of resources, so life's certain inclement weather can pass you by. This is a necessary trait for a black man, given that very few opportunities just befall us. Success has to be taken in many cases, so cherish the black man who boldly inserts his dreams in a society where governing bodies cherish his struggle and demise.

This mentality will transcend the family structure and increase his level of drive and productivity as your family increases in number. He will always consider his wife and family before himself, with his family unit serving as a motivating factor to get what is his daily for the furthering of his family's security.

Abundance is Him

The successful black man values financial abundance, but he does not make it the cornerstone of his existence and identity as a man. He is savvy and thoughtful toward his money, ensuring that abundance is his reality. His definition of himself as a successful man weighs on his principles and how he conducts himself on a daily basis. He doesn't rely on money to make him successful; instead, he relies on taking the best version of himself through life daily as the cornerstone of his definition of success.

His satisfaction in life is contingent upon him having the experiences he wants on a consistent basis, not with a pile of money stacked to the ceiling. His identity is not in the material world, meaning, he is solid through and through, regardless of any financial climate that may befall him. He's not afraid to take a loss, because whatever he lost is a byproduct of his essence that allowed him to create the various gains he accumulated throughout his life. He doesn't allow anyone or anything to impose a definition of him that is grounded in anything concerning the material world. His perception of himself is never in flux, as he stands tall on the core essence that is him.

The reversals of life never cause him to panic, rather to look to his source, God, and acknowledge the talents and abilities he's been given to change any situation to a favorable outcome. He views abundance not through the definition of worldly accumulations; he is abundance as he understands that worldly accumulations are a byproduct of him and his essence that allowed him to combine his talents with internal drive, energy, and diligent focus that culminated into a life of abundance.

He Has Decided

The successful black man is not perfect, nor will any human being ever be who walks the face of the earth. He simply decided what kind of man he is going to be, and evolved through his mistakes, while continuing to better himself daily. A solid man makes a declaration as to the type of man that he is going to be. His declaration is his compass. No worldly influences or pleasures dissuade him from being the man that he simply has made up in his mind that he is going to be. What many men find difficult to not entertain, he will bypass with the greatest of ease. If he has a woman in his life that enhances his overall wellbeing and experiences, there is nothing on this planet that can appeal to him more than her.

He influences the world around him, and the world around him does not influence him. I hope that you can begin to see what the makeup of a solid man consists of, and the importance of having this rock in your life. He simply has a code, which consists of the insights he has amassed through his life experiences, only incorporating what he believes are the best practices gleaned from his wisdom that make him the best version of himself. He will not come to you perfect, rather elevated and evolved. You can trust his guidance, as he has mastered himself and will add clarity and increase to the life of his woman and those closest to him. He will easily and always consider you first when faced with anything that can jeopardize the strength of your relationship. He's made enough mistakes to understand that best version of himself with his woman is one that without ceasing considers the woman across from him, while protecting and strengthening the bond you two possess in every moment.

He is Humble

The only way to arrive at the place of consciousness I describe this man of possessing is through extreme humility. He is evolved because he has acknowledged his wrongs and his contributions to unfavorable outcomes in life. He is a man of increase because he is strong enough to acknowledge his faults, and conscious enough to make declarations as to the type of man he will be moving forward in life after facing himself throughout the situations of life.

This humility will create a consistent balance between you two. He will examine himself first in any and all circumstances. His humility will allow him to admit his faults as you two progress together. His wisdom will allow him to show you, as gently as the circumstance calls for, where you could operate better for more favorable outcomes moving forward.

He Will Love and Respect You

His reverence for you fuels him to examine himself first and effortlessly love and respect you. This level of love and respect is given because you came packaged in a way that made him feel safe in allowing his emotions to progress to this point with you. Love and respect are cornerstones in the makeup of the man he has decided he will be. You inspire him to express and freely give those to you, given that you fit within the frame of the woman he can healthily co-exist with. The evolution into this woman happens with every turn of the page in this book.

You Can Follow Him

A man does not deserve to be followed unless his wisdom has consistently elevated your quality of life over time.

The successful black man is introspective and always willing and looking to grow. Consequently, he is wise, and is an asset to you if you submit to his wisdom, only when it is proven through personal increase in your life.

If you give this man reverence, and you respect his desire to increase you through his wisdom, it will be effortless, as he understands the power of having you at optimal levels of thinking and awareness. His results that he created for his life, before you two ever met, indicate that this man is calculated and intelligent, as he's elevated himself and his lifestyle consistently over time.

He understands that just because he may have education, worldly accumulations, societal standing, and solid career footing, he should not be automatically followed. His identity is no based on those things, so the entitled thought that women should automatically follow him just because he rose above the unfavorable realities that plague many black men, does not exist. He lives life from the inside out and not from the outside in, through validation by meaningless societal benchmarks and accumulations. This is what makes his wisdom true and ever expanding. He sees the material world for what it is: fleeting and naturally unstable. Since his identity is not in the material world he consistently evolves and improves, as he understands that the more intelligent and aware he becomes, he will influence life in the manner he desires and create the life that is ideal to him.

> **The successful black man will pour into you intellectually and spiritually in an unparalleled way, given that he sees life through a spiritual lens, which has translated to superior intellect.**

He can see things in this natural world that many are blind to. His wisdom will go before you. He will be the man that will not help you exclusively in the present; his wisdom will go before you and show you the snares and pitfalls in the future, while helping you to avoid them. This is the unparalleled wisdom I am referring to. When he opens your eyes to the future, through assessing situations accurately and precisely, he is to be followed without question.

His perspective of you is that he is no greater than you in a relationship. He respects the submission of his significant other, while respecting her enough to consider her thoughts pertaining to the various elements and situations of life. He understands that his significant other can increase him as well. He passionately pours wisdom into you with the understandings that the stronger you are spiritually and intellectually, the more secure and without encroachment the space you two will possess.

He Can Be Your Show Piece

Yes, the successful black man cares about his appearance. He always will represent himself in the best possible light. He understands style and chooses the one best suited to his individual preferences. He has a "look."

He will represent himself, and you, in the best possible light. He is not defined by his appearance, but understands the importance of reflecting the successful, vision oriented and perpetually achieving man that he is. He takes immense pride in himself, and subsequently his attire will always reflect that.

This is the man you will be proud to stand beside in many facets, with his appearance being one of them. He can be your "show piece." His well-groomed and stylish appearance will make him noticeable; his aura and energy will make him irresistible.

He Acknowledges His Source

As wise and knowledgeable as this man is that I describe, he understands he is nothing without the Creator who manifested him here and blessed him with wisdom, knowledge, and understanding. God is his source, and he humbly, willingly, and unashamedly acknowledges God as so in his life. This is the man you can safely submit to, the man who is submitted to God.

He has a solid spiritual foundation, so he will pray concerning issues between you two as his first resort to resolution. He will look to God to cover you both at every stage in your relationship. He proceeds through life with a God consciousness, which makes him aware, conscious, intelligent, calculated, and not rash in his decision making. He has a sense of purpose given that he acknowledges the Creator of the universe granted him a stay on earth. He is seeking the woman who will provide the healthy, balanced, and safe atmosphere that will allow him to continue to flow freely in his purpose and be the blessing to his fellow man he is designed to be. He wants his life enhanced, not detracted from.

Given that he is God centered, his life is in balance. He understands that no matter what station in life he currently resides, if he does his part, God will continue to increase him. No inclement weather rattles him. He is connected to the Source of all creation, and he possesses the perpetual confidence that reflects this level of trust in his Creator.

God is his rock, so he can be your rock no matter what life throws your way. If he is breathing, he will never see an obstacle as insurmountable, because God has empowered him to face all of life's challenges head on. He is fearless because his God is omniscient and all-powerful. His faith is not in himself; it is in the Creator of all.

This is what keeps him balanced and humble. He understands that every favorable experience he's lived came at the expense of his efforts and the favor of God in his life. This gives him perspective that keeps him humble, never succumbing to the temptations to glory in himself and his accomplishments. Pride may creep in because he is a human being, but it will not linger for long, as he praises his Source for all of life's increases. Every area of his life is influenced and guided by God. This is the man you and your children can have a safe existence with. He submits to his Creator without ceasing.

He Exists

Societal programming says black men are gay, dead, incarcerated, undereducated, and underemployed. There are many well put together successful black men that exists. I personally have a solid friend base of young 30 and 40 something educated/non-educated, hardworking, fruitful, and progressive black male friends. These friends do not just settle for their corporate salaries. Many of them have high profile professions with six figure salaries, while possessing rental properties, investment portfolios, and other businesses. This man typically isn't highlighted in society because it's a threat to the toxic narrative that is in play regarding us. But, yes, we do exist.

He Fancies The Black Woman

The matrix also wants us to buy into the narrative that the highly successful black man is married to women of other races, while valuing them above black women in totality. This statistic alone debunks that foolishness. In 2019, researchers Ivory A. Toldson of Howard University and Bryant Marks of Morehouse College conducted a study based on U.S. Census information. The study found that black men who make six figure salaries and higher marry black women at a rate of 85 percent, with 15 percent of these affluent black men marrying outside of their race. Black men who make less than six figures married black women at a rate of 75 percent, with 15 percent of these less affluent black men marrying outside of their race.

The study concluded that the large majority of financially successful black men prefer to marry black women. The more financially successful the black man is, the more likely he is to marry a black woman.

He is out there. By he, I am referring to the mythical successful black man that the powers want us to think doesn't exist. He is not only out there; he wants nothing more than to partner with his beautiful, black queen. He likely put up an amazing fight to achieve his respective level of success, so he needs you to be the best possible version of yourself, capable of being his peace in the midst of life's inevitable storms he faces due to the societal displeasure of him making it past where they said he should be. With every turn of the page in this book, you will become the woman he fancies.

Notes and Insights

Notes and Insights

Chapter 2

Find A Sound Minded Woman Mentor

Many young women do not have the luxury of a sound minded woman mentor in their lives to assist in guiding their steps. This became apparent in a conversation I had with an elder woman in our community. In this conversation, the woman said she never guided her daughters in relation to how to successfully prepare for and interact with a good and successful man. Her excuse was that her mother never showed her, as her mother was the primary provider for the household and focused on her work. My lack of understanding and displeasure with explanations like these is that by this point in your life you've had enough experiences with men, both good and bad, to pass on sound wisdom to your teen/twenty/thirty something year old daughter to imbed a mindset in her that will make her appeal to a successful black man.

Chris Broussard, the decorated Fox Sports sportscaster revealed a startling statistic in regard to black women and marriage in 2019. He said that 28 percent of all black women are projected to get married. This number, of 72 percent, of black women who are projected to go unmarried is an epidemic proportion. The cavalier and non-urgent approach from mothers to their daughters regarding the preparation of the daughter to function healthily in a relationship and marriage is not acceptable. The elder black women in the black community could benefit the younger black women exponentially if they chose to share their wisdom. Black marriage and healthy black images of marriage are paramount to setting healthy norms for black children, who represent our future leaders of our race. This passing on of wisdom is a nonnegotiable and must be approached with urgency if we are to reverse this cycle of non-black marriage amongst black women.

Take Responsibility

As a young black woman, you do not have the luxury of playing the blame game in terms of no one preparing you to function in a healthy relationship that could translate to a fulfilling marriage. More than likely, your crew of single girlfriends doesn't possess the acumen or life experiences necessary to help develop you into the woman that a successful black man would anxiously gravitate toward.

With this being said, you must possess the humility to seek out a sound minded woman mentor who will aid in your growth and progression to become the calibrated match for the successful black man. It's an incredible act of humility to admit that you don't have all the answers in life, and therefore, you seek people and information to help you positively progress.

The beautiful thing about this is that humility always lends way to incredible increase, whereas pride leads to a diminished life experience in the area it is exercised.

You must ask yourself how much you desire to be with the good men who enter your life. If the good, desirable men who enter your life continuously slip through your grasp, then your lens must focus back on you as to what they are seeing in you that doesn't compel them to explore you further. On a fundamental level, the man could see very quickly in the interaction between the two of you that he was not getting whatever he was putting into the interaction.

I personally have countless examples of women who have copped pleas after they did something with no rhyme or reason in the interaction that was a turn off, and purely ill advised. As a black woman, you don't know how many together black men are going to enter your space; the type of man you can build a fulfilling life with. The best thing that you could possibly do is to accept the responsibility of preparing yourself for this man that I describe. The successful black man who enters your space can be the one you grow with, or the one who got away. The choice is yours.

I'm not here to preach scarcity or fear. This is reality. It pains me to see young black women I'm interested in, who have shown me too many glaring red flags, come back and explain their displeasure and regret for their actions in our interaction. When I'm put in those positions, I must do the intelligent thing based on what I saw and keep myself removed from their space, given the gravity of what was revealed. Had these women had the right woman in their life to show them the way in dealing with men, I know in my heart, based on my level of interest and desire for these women, we could have easily gone the distance. Take the responsibility and find that sound minded woman mentor. Her guidance will serve you and take potential regrets and turn them into tangible and perpetual fulfillment. Make no excuse in finding her. You don't have the choice to not find her if the women in your life have a continuum of terrible results when dealing with men. It's up to you to seek her out. When you earnestly seek, you will find.

Who Should Be Your Mentor

Your mentor should be a woman who has a track record of results in their relationship life that you desire to replicate in your life. Their menu of results should entice you to want to experience every item on their menu. Your mentor will not have a perfect marriage, as no one does, but you will see longevity and connectivity between your mentor and her husband. You don't know who this person will be. It can be a family member, a co-worker, or a woman you observe from afar who has a genuine and fulfilled energy exchanging between her and her husband. Keep your eyes open for the fulfilled woman in her marriage and seek her out. I'm emphasizing the married woman because the man saw enough in this woman to desire nothing but her for the rest of his life. This woman conducts herself a certain way to have the faith and trust of a successful black man for a lifetime.

How To Approach Your Mentor

Respectfully approach your mentor and state your intentions to be mentored by them. Leave no mystery as to why you chose them. Point blank state your admiration for them and the desire you have to experience the results they've accumulated in their life. If the mentor decides to mentor you, then make yourself available to them so you can accumulate knowledge from them. Be proactive in establishing a great relationship with them by initiating contact and being a steady presence in their life. You have everything to gain in this situation, as this person has found and is experiencing the things you want to experience with men. As the relationship progresses, they will be free with their wisdom and give you more access to them, to the point where you can run scenarios and situations by them in real time. This is where their value really stands true. They can be the lifeline you need to conduct yourself in a manner that will not dissolve a good interaction with a good man through erratic and irrational behavior.

Don't Fight Them

It makes no sense to combat your mentor, as they are sharing the wisdom with you that you sought them out for. They have a complete menu of success. Listen to and apply their wisdom to your life. Their wisdom, when implemented, will make you appeal to the right type of black man, and subsequently allow you to recreate their success. The wisdom and guidance of your mentor is invaluable.

Often times the mentor is so fulfilled that they are not looking for anything in return. Their fulfillment comes from your evolution through the application of their knowledge. Their pay from you is that you value their guidance to the degree that you implement it into your life and begin to see the results in your life that drew you to them.

Your mentor is going to see things in you that are responsible for you not having achieved the various things in life you desired. They're going to call you out on certain thoughts and behaviors. Please do not be defensive when this happens. This is a necessary component for your growth and evolution into the type of person you want to be. If you continuously fight your mentor's reproach and knowledge, they will not be your mentor for long. They've already made a successful life in the area of life you desire to become successful in. If you are not receptive, they will depart due to the unnecessary frustration in their already fulfilled life.

It may hurt to have to examine yourself once your insufficiencies are brought to your awareness. See it as necessary and embrace the opportunity to change and to evolve. Exercise humility and understand that if certain things inside of you didn't need to be corrected, there would be no need for the mentor's presence in your life.

Evolve

The power in the wisdom from your mentor is when you understand that you need them because your way of thinking and moving through life has left your desires unattained.

Don't just listen to and apply the wisdom from your mentor, understand the way of thinking and logic that supports what they're saying. Seek the philosophy of your mentor. The philosophy is what gives power to the words. Once you adopt a philosophy that transcends the philosophy you possess that has made your desires elude you, your thinking will change, as well as your life.

There's a benefit to applying wisdom. The maximum benefit is in adopting the thinking behind the wisdom, which is the philosophy of your mentor.

The wisdom becomes earth shattering when you get the understanding behind the wisdom. That understanding will change your thinking. Once your thinking has elevated and changed, you have evolved.

The Full Experience

The full experience of mentorship is experienced when you are receptive to the knowledge and wisdom being given to you as I've previously explained. In addition to this, the mentor must be willing to give the full amount of knowledge and wisdom over time based on your level of commitment and consistency in receiving your mentor's guidance.

Your mentor will be watching you. You must also watch your mentor. I've had experiences where I was showing up the right way and the mentor was threatened by my gifts in a way that they feared I would surpass them. When this fear is present, the mentor cannot give their all, and you will not experience the full benefit of mentorship.

You have to pay attention to see if the person you desire to be your mentor is secure within themselves. In reality, you may be more attractive, have more education, and access to a more exclusive dating pool of men than they do.

The purity of the giving and receiving of wisdom has to be in place to receive the full experience of mentorship.

Pay attention and choose wisely. Make sure that your mentor knows that their presence is valued. Make sure you know that your presence is fully welcomed. If these elements are in place, your evolution into the type of black woman that can blow the mind of a successful black man will undoubtedly take place. The sound minded woman mentor will create a sound mind in you, and you will experience sound results in your life.

Mentor Yourself

No experience has to be wasted. Every interaction and relationship that doesn't work out leaves a wealth of information behind to help you understand yourself and evolve. The central theme of mentorship throughout this chapter has been personal evolution. You can evolve and grow tremendously if you take inventory of what your contribution was to the disassembling of your relationship. This requires you to take a hard look at yourself and choose to accept your involvement in why things didn't work out. At this point, when you identify your character flaws that were present, you now have the choice to face those flaws and make a declaration that you will not move in that manner moving forward in relationships.

You also will need to take a hard look at the other person and acknowledge any disheartening and toxic behaviors they presented to the relationship. Make a declaration that you will not tolerate those behaviors moving forward in your interactions with men. Once you identify these unfavorable behaviors and characteristics, you will easily be able to identify them moving forward.

You cannot control what you encounter, only what you allow into your space. Personal growth is a different response to the same situations. If you take internal and external inventory after unfavorable experiences with men, and accept the truth of what you see, and make declarations that facilitate the same behaviors and movements not being present in the next interaction you have with a man, you will react differently when placed in a similar position moving forward, and experience a drastically different and more favorable result.

Life serves us by consistently dealing us the same situations over and over again. It's okay when you don't have the knowledge to avoid unfavorable situations and outcomes when you encounter certain scenarios in life. When life deals you the same situation again, because it will, now you can apply the knowledge and wisdom you gained from the previous similar situation and react differently. This reaction brings about a more favorable outcome. This favorable outcome occurs because you chose to evolve and take away from the previous situation and not have the situation take away from you.

The Truth Will Set You Free

When you see individuals consistently experiencing unfavorable relationship outcomes, it's because they are refusing to stare at the truth of why the relationship did not work, and subsequently miss the advantage of evolving into the person who will not repeat those experiences. Many people don't possess the emotional maturity to stare at themselves and accept responsibility when things crumble in relationships. These are the people who will lie to themselves and always cast blame on others. The reality is that they are the constant in each situation.

The truth will set you free. The antithesis to this: the lie will keep you in bondage. Choose to evolve, and your relationship experiences will improve and heighten as you progress through life. The introspective and rational woman exudes beauty from the inside out. If you can self correct and exhibit prolonged positive changes in your life in areas that were once not healthy and unfavorable, you will blow a man's mind. This will command reverence and respect from the successful black man.

Notes and Insights

Notes and Insights

Chapter 3

Consider The Source

If someone is offering you advice pertaining to dating and all facets of male/female interaction dynamics, take a hard look at the reality of that person's life in that regard, and decide if you'd like to recreate their results. Emotion must be removed from the analysis of the results that a person has who is offering you advice. If you accept the wrong advice it will undoubtedly ruin the opportunity to experience healthy relationships with good men. You may revere, respect, and love the people who are offering you advice, but your fixated filter must be the results that they have in their life.

This is critical because you will recreate the results of the people you allow to speak into your life regarding relationships. This filter is to gauge what will be beneficial and what will detract from your desire to have a long withstanding and healthy relationship with a successful black man.

In Real Time

There was a situation within eyeshot of me regarding a young, beautiful black woman who was involved with a very good, young hard-working black man. The sentiment from the older black women around her was that she was too successful to deal with him.

These women were significantly older than her and were divorced or had never been married. This particular young black woman was strong minded and emotionally mature enough to continue to grow with this particular young black man. Over the course of time, she continued to accumulate academic credentials, becoming more decorated and made significant strides toward a very prestigious career path. This particular young black man, although he did not share his woman's academic accolades or societal value trajectory, continued to elevate himself personally and professionally. They supported and inspired one another, with the young lady drowning out the noise and taking a practical look at the opinions of the women around her who had landed in unfavorable positions with men and see things through an intelligent and practical lens.

This successful young black woman's decision to be true to what she observed about this successful young black man allowed her lens toward him to be uninhibited. It allowed her to see him for who he truly was: a man who desired nothing more than her; he adored, loved, and revered her. He was a man who would do anything for her, and he displayed his love and devotion to her over a prolonged period of time. He simply was proven.

These two young black love birds have since wed and are both very successful in their own right. They are completely engrossed in one another and have evolved into an admirable unit. They are a walking inspiration to any and all young and seasoned black people alike. They are each other's backbone and biggest cheerleaders.

All of this was made possible through this beautiful, educated, ambitious woman's ability to stay fixated on what the man across from her was in reality, as opposed to what the women in her life, who were unsuccessful with men, painted him to be. She simply considered the many sources who presented foolish information to her regarding the man who was her eventual husband.

This is easy. There are going to be great men who enter your life. Accompanying this will be one million opinions regarding this man as a good or bad fit for you. Simply consider the source, and you will always have perspective relating the man who is facing you. The people who offer you advice pertaining to the men in your life are dispensing information based on their personal philosophy. A person's philosophy embodies who they are, and explains every intricate detail of their life, both favorable and unfavorable.

This is where the implementation of the intelligent filter is paramount. If you take this filter with you when evaluating the opinions presented to you regarding the men who enter your life, you will avoid regret and live with the satisfaction of selecting the men who will give you the fulfilling life you desire.

The Only Time

The only time it is acceptable to internalize advice from someone who has undesirable relationship outcomes is when they are genuinely telling you to do the opposite of what they did so you can experience the opposite reality of what they experienced.

Pay attention to these people because it takes a selfless and humble person to help you move in a positive direction when they received negative results in the area of relationships.

The pain of a wrong decision, coupled with the acceptance of the responsibility for experiencing the pain, yields unparalleled depth of knowledge and wisdom.

This wisdom is not to be taken lightly.

Acknowledge God and His omniscience. This wisdom usually surfaces when the wrong opinion has surfaced in your space and is becoming influential. Pay attention to the sequences surrounding the timing of wisdom that is presented to you. Evolve to the point where you can easily recognize what is in front of you and have clarity in deciphering if the information is worth internalizing, or better left not considered.

Be Admirable

It's admirable when a young black woman can filter through nonsense and easily see the great qualities of the man who is in front of her. This ability by the young woman is rooted in strength and personal clarity. It exudes a maturity that will make a man of intelligence and reason respect you. It's admirable when you don't have to play from behind in a relationship and come back to a good black man copping pleas after you realize the error in your movements that resulted from you accepting the wrong advice from the wrong people. The successful black man will appreciate this. Your mental strength will make you a fixture in his thoughts of his future life when he sees you can intelligently process information and keep the wrong influences outside of the space that you two possess together.

You can get it right on the front end. You don't have to continuously repel the blessings that are sent your way. Make getting it right initially when it comes to good men your intention and practice in life.

A weak woman cannot be trusted by a successful black man.

> **Having a woman whose mind is easily influenced is a detriment to the overall security and quality of life of the successful black man.**

The Best Version of You

When you consistently ingest uplifting messages that speak to valuing yourself and being the healthiest version of yourself mentally, spiritually, and emotionally, inaccurate and negative information regarding the good men in your life will be put into its proper perspective, having no influence over you whatsoever. It's great to negate this misinformation on a fundamental level of just considering the results of the person in front of you who is disseminating false information to you regarding good men. The advanced approach is to be so fully aware of yourself, and what you desire in a man, that you can automatically decipher who this man in front of you, is to you, in his totality. When positive and negative opinions are voiced to you concerning him, they are all irrelevant because the healthy relationship you have with yourself and your desires constantly reveals who this man is. It's as if you'll have on armor that cannot be penetrated by false and negative opinions regarding the good men that enter your space.

It is great when you can ride off into the sunset with the type of man who will love, cherish, respect, revere, and encourage you for a lifetime. It's a tremendous weight to carry through life when you know that a man did all the right things and you let him go due to opinions draped in the negative contributions people have made to their own relationship demises. Be solid and be strong. Love, cherish, and understand yourself enough to immediately identify who is showing up in your space and in your life. Playing with a lead is much easier than playing from behind. Work on yourself without ceasing and be the match for the successful black man who wants nothing more than to encounter you.

Notes and Insights

Notes and Insights

Chapter 4

Don't Make Him Work For It

Typically, this phrase has a sexual connotation to it, but I'm referring to "work" in the holistic sense with no particular emphasis on one facet of the interaction with a man. Making a man work for you, in any regard, implies that you are the prize. Any successful and centered man will not view anyone above or beneath him. In reality, "He has to work for me" establishes a very unhealthy dynamic.

Relationship Dynamics

The intelligent black man understands that the dynamic that is established in the beginning of the interaction is the one that permeates the entire relationship. He will literally spend the rest of his life, if you two are married, catering to you of he accepts this lopsided dynamic. The successful black man has no interest in continually giving, with the actions and essence not being reciprocated to him. When a woman says or implies this to me, I'm gone, quickly.

> **If a man values himself, he won't be able to engage in an interaction where he is not receiving whatever he is giving.**

I am 36 years old. I've had the luxury of seeing friends my age complete the cycle of marriage and divorce. I respectfully asked them about the dynamics that caused the collapse of their marriage. In unison, they all say that the unhealthy dynamics that existed in the beginning pervaded the entire relationship, and the gravity of the dynamic worsened. In one of my friend's words, "I saw the red flags, but chose to see the good in her." Everything that contributed to the demise of his marriage was very present from the beginning of the interaction.

I've had these experiences as well with lopsided dynamics in relationships I've engaged in. The very things I overlooked in the beginning only intensified, ultimately to the point that I had to examine what my life would be like if I continued. The difference between some of my friends and I, however, is that I simply got out of the situation before it turned into anything beyond a relationship.

> The successful black man is cerebral. You don't become successful as a black man without being calculated, intelligent, and deductive in your thinking.

He is watching everything. If you match his energy and effort and establish that mutual respect will be the foundation of your relationship he will appreciate this, as the way you move is a severe departure from the entitlement he is consistently greeted with by women.

Lose The Entitlement

With the amount of black women who will never marry existing in epidemic proportion, entitlement is the last approach you should take in an interaction with a successful black man. How can you rationalize only 28 percent of black women ever getting married, with: this well put together, hard-working, intelligent black man owes me something, and we don't even know each other? It's foolish to think his way. If this is your stance, someone has failed you. I'm here to give you a chance to build the life that you desire with the type of man that fits within that frame, if this is what you desire for yourself.

I pray that you value yourself as a black woman because you are the most awe-striking creature that I have ever laid eyes on. You just do it for so many black men, effortlessly, in terms of our desire for something so divine. Within this reality, you don't want to overplay your hand and over value yourself. Keep your mind fixated in reality and you will get the results you want with the type of man that you desire. Entertain delusion and you will be left wondering "what happened" as time passes you by.

Peaceful Dynamics

The successful black man does not want to contend with the rigors of always having to cater to you, with relationship undertones of "what have you done for me lately?"

He desires the smooth experience entrenched in mutual reverence and respect as the basis of the interaction, which translates to an effortless evolution with you over time.

He's fought to create a peaceful and stable life for himself, and he has reconciled that if he doesn't find the woman who he can maintain this way of living with, he is fine with that. It's a win/win for him. If he finds her, he wins, as he maintains his quality of life. If he doesn't find her, he wins because he maintains his quality of life. It's really that simple in his mind. He's clear on and in himself. His decisions are precise, calculated and reasonable. If you greet him with entitlement, he will thank you for revealing yourself so early on, and politely remove himself from your space.

The Rules Don't Apply

You want to do away with rules and go with the energy of the interaction. This is natural and enjoyable. If a black man has become successful, he likely had to be decisive, analyze many situations quickly, and lean on his instincts. A man in this position sees rules as a detriment to the very way of moving that is responsible for his success.

It's appealing to a man when a woman can easily move in the interaction according to the mutual energy that you share, as opposed to disrupting this natural flow and energy with rules. Being able to move according to the energy and connection that you share is indicative of emotional maturity. Not many men can reflect and say they encountered an abundance of women who didn't introduce unnecessary rules and games into the equation. You, being the woman who flows naturally, represent a departure from what he's used to experiencing with women. This will make him gravitate toward you with anticipation.

Not everything happens on timelines and schedules. You may meet a man and date him for months and not develop intense attraction or experience the spark that makes you anticipate his presence. Contrarily, you may meet a man that you are completely immersed in after one encounter. That's the beauty in being present and acknowledging the energy you share with someone. The flow is uninhibited, and you can both focus on the reality of the connection, instead of expending valuable energy trying to figure out an interaction that is reminiscent of a jigsaw puzzle.

Express Yourself

Many women are surprised at how forthcoming I am about what I want from an interaction, and my ability to express my feelings to a woman as they are developing. They say many men hold back.

I say to these women that I am man enough to tell you how I feel on the front end and act accordingly, so I don't have to mess things up knowing how I feel about you, and be in a position where I finally express my true feelings on the back end. In essence, why complicate a situation that could be simple and effortless?

Many women speak of guys who didn't express their feelings on the front end, and as the woman's emotional investment in the interaction wanes, he then articulates his emotions concerning her. I tell women that it's actually weak to engage in something on a false premise. If a man is into you, at whatever level, he should express that and not be afraid of how it makes him look. A real man can move this way, because he has no fear of losing any woman. He understands it moves the relationship along in a healthy manner when it is established that the feelings and emotions that exists are mutual.

Many men feel validated in their manhood by not expressing how they feel to women as things are developing between them. The truth is that they always reveal them, but often times it's on the back end when they face the threat of losing the woman they are into. The bottom line is that emotions will be expressed at some point by the man, the type of man he is dictates when these emotions will be communicated to the woman he fancies.

The successful black man lives to win and not to lose. The woman who is calibrated to him lives in the same manner. These two individuals meeting and progressing in a relationship in a manner where they are both true to themselves, sets the stage for real magic to be an ever-present entity in their relationship. The greatest strength is in vulnerability. The most life altering experiences do not happen on timelines and schedules.

Those Rare Moments

Those rare moments I am referring to are when you meet someone who blows your mind and encapsulates your thoughts, with the feeling being mutual. Most people do not meet many people who fit these criteria regularly. This experience may elude you over the course of years, or it can happen unexpectedly as you are exiting a lengthy relationship. It happens when it happens; but the frequency of this level of connection is rare.

In order to capitalize on these moments, you want to be available and engaged with no inhibitions. This does not mean that your eyes aren't open in terms of observing the person across from you. You must always be observant of people, as this is the intelligent way to move through life. Being able to engage in these moments fully is based on your ability to trust yourself.

Trust Yourself

Your ability to trust yourself, and fully engage in situations with men that are enjoyable, is based on how you dealt with your previous situations with men. If you took away from the situations and examined yourself afterwards, along with taking a hard look at the man you were involved with, you tend to emerge from the situation more evolved and aware of yourself. If you played the blame game without acknowledging your shortcomings in the interaction, or you just moved on without taking any inventory of your actions or the man's actions, then you missed the opportunity to grow, and likely developed baggage that will make you hesitant in the presence of the man who could hold the key to a healthy relationship.

> **The people who take away from relationships, and don't allow relationships to take away from them, engage in their next interaction open, while traveling very light due to the absence of baggage.**

Games, gimmicks, and rules are not present in this person's world due to the ability to trust their own discernment of people based on their life experiences and subsequent evolutionary knowledge that they acquired at the hands of it.

The successful black man has done this. He does not delegate blame wrongly. He stares himself in the face and is always open to bettering himself through personal improvement. He is expecting you to show up the same way. Fifty games and fifty rules are not his ideal experience, and he will quickly disengage when this is present. All rules go out of the window when you trust yourself.

The Barometer

Instead of rules and games being your barometer and precedent when dealing with a man, let it be the observation of whether you are receiving the same energy that you are extending to the man. When you take a mentally healthy approach to dating you are observing your level of emotion that is developing in the interaction as well as the reciprocation of energy that you are expending.

The choice to move forward with the person you are involved with is simple when this is your precedent in the interaction. If the person is putting in what you're depositing into the interaction, you move forward. If they are not, then you exit stage left. It's really that simple.

Having this barometer comes at the expense of having self-respect and self-awareness. You are fully present and are looking at the person across from you through a lens of understanding and respecting yourself. Games, gimmicks, and rules are indicative of insecurity and emotional immaturity. The choice to evolve through every experience by taking inventory and unpacking the situation leaves your mind and being elevated. When you are elevated, you don't elicit or engage in silly stuff. The people who do literally turn you off. That's what this chapter is about: presenting an aware and healthy minded version of yourself to the successful black man so he recognizes the gem that you are, and views getting to know you and progressing as a pleasure, rather than a detriment.

The only people who allow or engage in games and other forms of disrespect and mistreatment are people who don't respect themselves.

No self-respecting and self-aware person stays in an unhealthy situation long enough to develop emotional baggage.

If you show up this way to a successful black man who has mastered his life and himself, your incompatibility will immediately present itself in the interaction, as you are bringing unhealthy baggage and ways of moving that will be glaringly evident, due to the fact that these elements are absent in his world. Always choose to evolve daily.

If constantly choosing to evolve and understand yourself is your mantra, you'll be in perpetual evolved state. This will be your space. The successful black man is introspective and not above reproach, so he exists in this space as well. When you two encounter one another, from the initial "hello," thoughts of "where have you been hiding?" will be the mutual sentiment. The energy, reverence, and anticipation for each other's presence will be undeniable. His decision to put one foot in front of the next through your effortless evolution will be one of the easiest decisions he has ever made.

Notes and Insights

Notes and Insights

Chapter 5

He Has To Have More Than Me

There are happy couples where the woman makes more money than her man. The best couples are in their own world and not influenced by societal norms and expectations concerning gender roles. There are lopsided disparities in salaries in the corporate world, with black women making more money than black men. This occurs by design. Corporate America is affectionately referred to as the corporate plantation by many famous black scholars who understand corporate dynamics.

The Corporate Plantation

When slavery existed in the United States this would have been my plight. I'm six feet five inches in height, and in the prime of my life at 36 years old, while possessing the build of a professional athlete. Once the slave owner purchased me from the auction block, I would have been taken back to his plantation. Upon my arrival, the other slaves would have seen me. With my height and build, I could have possibly represented leadership and hope for the existing slaves. I could have been a representation of someone who could be rallied behind, and this level of hope in oppression based controlled environments, must be immediately neutralized.

Once the slave owner hears the whispers and sees the slaves' sentiment toward me, he would promptly have everyone stop what they're doing and gather around. I would be tied and beaten to the point of near death, and possibly compromised in other demeaning ways so the owner could make the statement that I could not be looked to for hope. I would be allowed to live because there's plenty of labor and reproductive value a slave like me would earn for the plantation owner. This likely would be my plight on a real plantation.

The corporate plantation is very similar. I would be emasculated as soon as I stepped foot through the doors with the boss letting everyone know who is in charge. As a collective, black women earn more than black men in corporate America, so the black men do not appeal to black women as suitable life partners. They're thinking is that if the black man is emasculated with his salary being lower than the black women he is surrounded by daily, he will not appear as a suitable partner in the mind of the black woman who out earns him.

This tactic is harmonious with the black man being removed from the house after the deaths of Martin Luther Ling, Jr. and Malcom X. Those men had too much control over the black consciousness and unified it to forward the race tremendously. The goal after their assassinations was to never have another "Martin" or "Malcom" rise up.

That successor would likely come from a two-parent black household where success was the norm and the foundation to become anything they desired to be was laid. Those children would also have a healthy image of black love and perpetuate the cycle of black marriage and creating children with a strong perception of themselves and black love.

The philosophy of the actual slave plantation and the corporate plantation are linear. If you are attracted to a black man and he has drive, ambition, is loving, and has the ability and desire to provide, he is your match, regardless of your societal standing and material acquisitions! The amount of available, educated, financially well-off black men is at a deficit in comparison to black women. It's basic supply and demand. Your net must be broadened, or you simply run the risk of not being married, if marriage to a man that has the qualities I articulate in this book, is your ideal ending.

> **You may have to bring the hard working, attractive trade guy to your corporate functions.**

He Will Find His Way

Not every black man is to be partnered with. Not every black man is to be followed. If the black man has not quite gotten his footing financially, and in life, one thing must be considered: his level of ambition. Here is my story of a relationship that I was involved in when I was on the cusp of financial freedom and prosperity.

I was in a relationship at a time in my life where I had been fighting for years to make a solid turn in my career in the self-development industry. I was diligent in this pursuit as I continued to write books, do public appearances, and take any and all opportunities that came my way that I believed would move me forward. I had been working a noncommittal full-time type of job not too long before I engaged in this relationship. I left it because I knew it was my time to go full-time into business for myself.

I was experiencing some waves of good financial times, interspersed with periods of still finding my way. I was fighting very hard every day when I entered this relationship. I had a few luxuries and evidence that my hard work had provided a sustainable lifestyle for me. Couple this with my hard working and consistent nature toward my craft, and it was safe to say that I had the makings of a man who would catch his stride and eventually find the footing that would financially set me up for life.

There were influences present early on in the relationship persuading the young lady that I was involved with that I was "less than," and would never amount to anything of substantial increase. I was not a safe bet. This was expressed to me from her very early on in the interaction from people who were divorced and participating in unhealthy relationships. When this was expressed to me, I simply kept going, never allowing my perception of myself to be lessened. I simply told the young lady that I could get any woman I wanted, and to not come at me in that manner again.

I continued to grow my business throughout this tumultuous relationship. The influences in the young lady's ear manifested repeatedly in our relationship, until the perception of the projected failure I would be overshadowed the reality of the hard working man that I was, with the results in my life moving in a positive direction. The relationship inevitably ended.

In the first thirty days after that relationship ended, everything that this young lady and the people around her were convinced would never transpire in my life did. In that thirty days I had my first $20,000.00 month of earnings. It wasn't earth shattering money, but it definitely signaled that I had entered a new realm of prosperity. From that time on, financial prosperity was a fixture in my life. I became everything that the young lady and people close to her never thought I would become.

Trust me when I say: He will find his way.

Full Circle

Years after this relationship ended, I was at an establishment doing a book signing. A lady in her mid-fifties to early sixties stopped by my table and was checking out my books. I told her what each one was about, but my books were not her interest. She pulled out her phone and showed me pictures of her daughter.

She explained to me how the man in her daughter's life, her fiancé, did not match her in educational accolades and degrees. They had a child together and the young man in her daughter's life was in school and progressing steadily toward his own academic accolades.

This couple was in their late twenties. In the mind of the woman who approached me, I was an upgrade for her daughter given I had an education and a flashy career as an author, motivational speaker, and entrepreneur. I promptly asked the lady some questions. I asked does this young man love, respect, and provide for your daughter? She responded with, "yes." Given he is exhibiting the signs of a provider, and he is steadily working to improve himself, does he exhibit and upward trajectory of success? She responded with, "yes."

I then explained that it takes a little longer for some black men to catch their stride in life, and quite frankly that this young man is your daughter's match. I explained what would happen if her daughter somehow found herself back in the dating pool. She would potentially lose a viable black male mate and the father of her child, forever. When that black man achieves his portion of success he's been fighting for, he will be rare and in demand with women. He's clearly on the horizon of this happening. He will be a successful, young, decorated, and very valuable dating option for many women. If your daughter lets him go for no clear reason, he will find the younger and prettier version of your daughter easily. And once he gets a steady taste of young, gorgeous women, your daughter will be in no man's land with him. He's gone.

Your daughter is approaching thirty. You want your daughter with a very successful man, but the men in her age range that have the level of success that your daughter has, and more, are dating the younger version of your daughter.

I simply reiterated, "Ma'am, your daughter has a great man in her life who has loved and cared for your daughter and their child over time. You also mentioned that your daughter loves this man. Please understand that this man is a match for your daughter, and convincing your daughter to engage in hypergamy, will likely backfire."

I wanted to see her daughter hold onto the young, black king who was a loving presence in her life, as well as their child's life. I was not there to tell this middle-aged woman any lies, and I am not here to deliver fabrication to you either. I hope she backed off of her daughter and gained a renewed appreciation and reverence for her eventual son-in-law that day.

This Type of Man

If you ridicule the type of man I just wrote about as "less than" as he is ascending in life, when God honors his diligence and he finally breaks through, resentment toward you may exist that he is incapable of moving past.

Never underestimate the value that a person has for themselves. It is a tremendous mental hurdle to overcome when you finally break through and become everything people thought you would never be, and have a

mindset to share the spoils of your war with people who told you that you weren't built for victory.

Honor and Respect Him

A real man is secure within himself no matter where he stands in his life's journey, as long as he is doing what he can to propel himself forward.

Extend a baseline of respect to the men you interact with who are trying and progressing. You never know what the man you are interacting with may become, and what you two can build together.

I have been blessed with a vantage point of seeing educated women with hardworking men, who don't share their same level of education, thrive together, creating beautiful families, and building a substantial net worth.

If the man has the baseline that I described in the book of what a successful black man should be, and you are attracted to him, give him a chance. Accept that your man may or may not come packaged the way society says he should be based on what you've accomplished and accumulated in your life.

There are levels of disrespect that make a relationship beyond salvaging. Celebrate your man as he is progressing. The successful black man will see you through the lens of exactly how you are showing up in his life, with no outside interference concerning the influences who attempt him to see you otherwise. If a man is not exactly where he wants to be in life, but maintains a healthy perspective of himself, you can cross a line of disrespect that cannot be recovered from, even if the man tries. I've been there. See the man in your life for who he is to you and how he consistently shows up in your life. You don't want to cross an unsalvageable line and look back with regret concerning a phenomenal man who escaped your grasp.

Develop Your Eye

There are many men who want nothing substantial for their lives. They're all talk, with no results. These men are in love with the idea of making you believe they are something that they know they are not. Gratification for this man is in the idea of being whatever he is portraying, and not in the reality of becoming that. I am in no way advocating for these men. Pastor R.C. Blakes said something very thought-provoking in a podcast I listened to. He alluded to a man showing signs of life in his aspirations by the time he is 30. If that man has been giving significant energy toward his craft or profession, at a certain point there should be fruitful results that accompany his ambition and effort. Do not fall for a silver tongue with no substance backing their claims; learn to see past a man's words into the realm of results that he has created for himself. If he is a real man, undertaking a substantive pursuit, he will have progress and results accompanying his aspirations.

Mental Strength

Many women miss out on good men because of their concern with the opinions and expectations of others. Society, your family, or your co-workers may condemn your decision to partner with a man who doesn't match your societal allure, but you must possess the mental and internal strength to be in your own world with the man you choose, while growing together and arriving at whatever destination life sets before you. We don't encounter an overabundance of genuinely happy people who love their lives. Choose whatever compels you to move forward with the man you desire and have that speak louder than voices who don't see your man the way you see him.

You want to join yourself with a man for the right reasons. This seems to be a foreign concept these days as what people can gain from the other person, and societal posturing is a common motive for unions. Be at one with yourself and acknowledge what the man is presenting to you, and the mutual energy that you share.

Fulfillment comes when you create your life, your way, while never being afraid to paint your vision on life's canvas.

Notes and Insights

Notes and Insights

Chapter 6

Size Him Up Accurately

You simply can not treat all men the same. No one is above or below anyone. Within that statement is the reality of market value. Market value determines a man's place within the dating pool. The man who is successful, cares about his appearance, is well-rounded, respected, in shape, secure within himself, and stands on morals and principles is the highest value male you are going to encounter.

This man's value, in terms of the dating market, is determined by how in demand he is with women. This type of man is out there, but in my observation, not in over abundance. His rarity sets his market value.

Contrarily, you have men who don't captivate women regularly. Typically, these are the men who just aren't clicking on all cylinders like the high value man. Maybe he's not that together in areas of his life where he could be better. Possibly there's an "it" factor that has eluded him. Whatever this man is missing is responsible for him being overlooked regularly by women.

Typically, this man is the one who will pursue you with no thought of his own self-respect. He'll inbox you repeatedly when you don't respond. He'll continue to try to talk to you in public when all social cues indicate that you are not interested. Women walk by him like he doesn't exist. These are men who have not tapped into what will focus them and give them a high value in the dating market. They are all encompassing undesirable men, especially when you include them into the conversation of the acquisition of extremely beautiful women.

Monopoly Money

These are the types of men that many women build their egos on. There's never a shortage of them who will over pursue women who aren't interested in them, making complete fools of themselves in the process. These types of men make women think that they can treat all men, any kind of way, and the man will stick around, because these men exist in such high numbers. These are the men who accommodate regular disrespect from women. They create a false reality that all men can be tossed around, and they'll still be patiently waiting for the woman he desires to come around.

The glaring issue is that most women who allow their egos to be inflated by undesirable men can't see the fallacy that is staring directly at them: These are men you do not desire, so it's as if they don't exist when they adorn your path with roses. In essence, their adoration is meaningless because the adoration is not coming from the men you actually desire. If there was an overabundance of high value men who regularly engage you, you would not be available. You'd be in a committed relationship or married.

Most women desire high value men. That's perfectly fine because they have made themselves into desirable men. Many women fail to acknowledge that although many men worship and adore them; typically, these are not the men that they are into. It's rare for most women to regularly meet men that they are encapsulated with. To get into an interaction with a man that you are actually into, you cannot treat this man the same way that you treat the many men who adore you that you are not interested in. They have self-respect and standards.

> **High value men treat women with respect and require this treatment in return. If you offer anything less than this to the high value man, he is gone, quickly.**

How To Be Appealing To Successful Black Men... For Black Women

If you desire to be with a man of high value, you must extend the same level of respect to him that he is extending to you. If you think that he is going to stick around for the same nonsense you dish out to the men you are not interested in, you are mistaken. This is the equivalent of attempting to spend monopoly money in a real store. That currency of entitlement, dismissive behavior, and disrespect only spends in places who accept fake currency. If you attempt to spend fake currency in a real store, you will promptly be removed from the premises.

I can't count how many times I've been respectful to women and they were more concerned with getting me under their spell, than acknowledging my footing in the dating pool. Their movement was in accordance with their inflated egos, and what they're used to. The unfortunate part about this is some of these women actually liked me; and I liked them as well, or I never would have approached them and expressed an interest. It's like Groundhog Day. The woman goes out of her way to do something disrespectful when no provocation occurred; I disappear, then the woman comes back asking what happened? What happened was that the woman attempted to spend monopoly money in a real store. It's better to recognize that you've encountered the high value man early on the interaction. Do not go through life interacting with every man the same, from the vantage of your falsely inflated ego. Exercise humility and actually size the man up in front of you so you know how to interact with him in a manner that he will want to stick around. If this is the type of man you desire, it's self serving to acknowledge that you're going to have to bring a respectful, engaged, and consistent version of yourself to him.

Solid High Value Men

A man is not high value because of his material acquisition and societal standing. He is high value because he values himself highly. Since he values himself highly and has a healthy perception of himself, he has acquired all of the societal decorations that are widely celebrated. He possesses those accolades; those accolades do not possess or define him. He is a solid man who has made a declaration of how he will move through life and treat people. Since he values himself, nothing can remain in his space that is not congruent with how he sees himself.

Many men act as if they move this way. I've been around some of coldest, supposedly heartless, self-proclaimed players that exist, only to find out that they are feminine and allow women to disrespect them all in the name of hopefully getting intimate with her. These are feminine men masquerading as real men. This is why the importance of acknowledging and posturing yourself to the high value masculine man is of great importance. The average man you encounter is feminine, and not the masculine man you innately desire to compliment your femininity.

There was a gentleman I met years ago who was the quintessential ladies' man. He had the height, the profession, looks, money and other enticing intangibles that appealed to a wide array of women. He is a cool guy, and I'm taking nothing away from him. Something occurred one day that made me view him differently in regard to his proclaimed unrelenting player classification.

I began dating a very beautiful woman. She informed me that she looked at my social media and we have a male friend in common that she dated briefly. Based on how gorgeous this woman was, I knew exactly who it was. I said his name and she laughed. I told her, "I know how this guy likes them!"

She then went on to tell me how he wined and dined her on several occasions, and constantly contacted her without her even responding to him. I couldn't believe this, but knowing the nature of most men, especially when it came to a woman possessing her awe-striking beauty, it was very plausible. She then went on to show me a string of non-responded-to text messages from the guy. As the popular terminology says: "She had receipts." This guy was the most unusual suspect to behave in this manner. This taught me that most men, regardless or their allure and status, compromise themselves when it comes to tolerating disrespect from women; and most women know that many men will tolerate deep levels of disrespect if they are attracted to a woman.

The issue is that you want to be with a man who is solid and that you can respect. You instinctively want a real man, even if you are not calibrated to receive him. You will always desire a solid man, because he will stand up to any challenge that you two may face, or the potential family that you will have with this man.

Given the rarity of this man, the best course of action is to be able to recognize him when he enters your presence, so you know how to treat him. This is the successful black man you can safely join yourself to, and know that he values himself and will give nothing but the absolute best version of himself to any women who he sees value in.

The material world has propped this black man up; but, he is not propped up by his material acquisitions and highly favorable societal posturing. He is the same man with or without society's high opinion of him due to what he accomplished. His validation resides in being an evolved, self-aware, absolute best version of himself. The high value black man understands that anything in the material world is fleeting. He's probably struggled at different stations along his life's journey. His value is in himself and can never be compromised. If you enter this man's space with the eye to recognize who he is, and you see him the same way that he sees himself, you will be poised for a great experience with a solid man who takes an exceptional version of himself through life.

Many men will adore you. It's only significant if adoration comes from this type of man.

The Rational Approach

Given the rarity of the type of men who are actualized enough to respect themselves without ceasing, while offering you that same level of respect, why mistreat him? The mantra amongst many young black women, due to media influence is, "He better approach me with a bag of money and I'm going to offer him whatever behavior suits my mood at any given time." In essence, many men are greeted with women who attempt to control, manipulate, extort, and disrespect them as their first course of action regardless of how the man shows up. The new definition of womanhood, in my observation, is that if you can proceed like this with any man, and they stick around for it, you are a top-notch woman that no one can touch.

Real womanhood is offering the man, who you are attracted to, the same level of respect, involvement, and consistency that he is offering you, without introducing fifty games into the equation in an attempt to establish yourself as the more valuable commodity in the interaction.

Womanhood is being so in tune with yourself that you never entertain the involvement of games, because if anything is not congruent from the man in regard to how you see your-

self, in addition to the way you have been treating him, you remove yourself from the situation.

This is real womanhood. Moving contrary to this will appeal to weak and insecure men who will tolerate this type of interaction, because they are calibrated to this low energy nonsense.

Take A Hard Look At Him

Given that women rarely meet men who they are attracted to and possess qualities that regularly enthrall women, this level of attraction toward a man is to be revered. If you seldom come across men who meet these criteria, it's guaranteed that when you do meet a man who is capable of encapsulating your thoughts, he possesses qualities that translate to mass appeal to women. If you find him rare, there are many other women who share your sentiment toward him. These women, regardless of how you may be celebrated daily for the best attributes you possess, have your attributes and more.

Just as adoration from men has been your consistent experience, extreme interest from a myriad of women is a fixture in his world. This is his level, as this is his consistent experience with women. He experienced it all and has access to it all, given the type of man that he's become, and rarity that accompanies the choices he made. His mindset pertaining to women is abundance, because abundance is his reality. He regularly gets approached by desirable and universally appealing women. Waitresses deliver phone numbers to him as he is leaving restaurants from women who were intrigued by his aura. This is real and happens consistently in real time. This is his reality.

When so many men adore and chase you, it's difficult to even entertain that any man, outside of a celebrity, has a parallel experience to you with the opposite sex.

> **I'm here to tell you that black men who arrive at certain stations in life have an access to women, that if you were aware of, you would never approach him as if you are the prize in the equation that comprises you two.**

I'm writing this to deliver a real perspective, so you can recognize this man when you encounter him, and so you can be a departure from what accompanies the women who he regularly interacts with.

The high value black man epitomizes substance. He's not enthralled with the amount of attention he gets from women, because that is a fixture in his world. He's more so anticipating meeting a woman of substance. The revelation of this woman begins in the beginning of the interaction when he can see that you are approaching him eye to eye, not demanding anything from him except that he shows up as the best version of himself, and treats you how you deserve to be treated. No looks, complexion, hair, money, or titles are at the focal point of this man's desire. He wants you, whole and respectful, so the exploration of what can be can proceed, as he recognizes you as a valuable commodity.

If you show up differently to this man, as if the world revolves around you, he'll scoff, and then keep it moving. He understands that in the abundance of women who make themselves available to him, one will eventually show up that he is extremely attracted to, who recognizes him for who he is. I guarantee, he'll park it right there.

The beginnings of the journey with the successful black man are in treating him exactly the way he is treating you: with integrity, respect, and anticipation of his presence. When entitlement, disrespect, and condescending tones become apparent early from a woman, the successful black man will see you as an avoidable and unnecessary headache. If you show up into this man's life with the perspective of his rarity, and understand how to move in his world in accordance to his reality as the incredible man he has become, you will be the welcomed breath of fresh air he's been anticipating. He will exhale.

Notes and Insights

Notes and Insights

Chapter
7
Be His Peace

The deciding factor that makes me desire a woman's presence is whether she will take away from my quality of life. Everyone has their contingencies. Peace is at the forefront of the life and lifestyle I have created for myself.

We're all equals. The woman across from me has the same right to weigh my presence against her desired intangibles that support the furthering of the life and lifestyle she enjoys.

The one recurring issue I've seen that has made me pump the breaks quickly in an interaction is mental health issues and unresolved trauma. We've all been through traumatic events in life. They've taken a toll on each one of us, to varying degrees. We all come out differently. It's important to evaluate our contributions that are made to failed interactions with people that we were interested in. The self-examination may unearth some commonalities in which we made unhealthy and consistent toxic contributions to interactions.

> **If the same version of us is taken through life to new situations and circumstances, the outcome will inevitably be the same.**

Embrace Mental Health

One of the most powerful and insightful social media videos of 2019 came from the wise and decorated black man, Will Smith. This video was titled: "Fault vs. Responsibility." In this video, Will Smith said that we've all been through unfortunate and traumatic life circumstances that weren't our fault, but it is our responsibility to deal with the residuals that manifest themselves in our life in unhealthy ways.

Every person is constructed differently, while having varying thresholds for dealing with trauma, and emerging with a sound mind. Some people endure circumstances that many wouldn't deem as life altering in nature, and they are damaged mentally and spiritually. Others experience situations that beg the question: "How in the world did you make it through that with your sanity?"

It's difficult to see exactly where you fit in that spectrum of life circumstances taking a mental and emotional toll on you, but at some point, if you continue to get unfavorable outcomes in dating and in life, the mirror must turn toward you. Even if you don't fully understand what you see, seek the help you need.

This help could be a mental health professional such a psychiatrist, counselor at church, or many other people of mental health vocations. What must be undertaken, on your behalf, is the quest to reverse the traumatic effects of simply existing for a prolonged period of life. This must be a necessity and approached with urgency. Your attitude and approach to dealing with the residuals of life's unfortunate experiences and circumstances determines how healthy and enjoyable of a life you will have. It also influences how you will show up as a potential mate for someone who is emotionally and mentally healthy.

What I like best about Will Smith's video is the emphasis on acknowledging that many things that happened to us were not our fault. If you're a child and adults introduce unhealthy circumstances that take a toll on you mentally and emotionally, that was completely out of your control and capacity of responsibility. Will Smith says regardless of the cause of the residuals of the trauma that introduces itself in your life, repeatedly, at the most inopportune times, it's your responsibility to take measures to restore yourself mentally and emotionally. It's not fair to have had to endure many circumstances that were beyond your control. An optimal quality of life is in the reconciliation that no, I shouldn't have endured certain toxic experiences in life, but my quality of life will be determined by how I emerge from those ashes. If you focus on taking responsibility for having the optimal experiences in life, you will be postured to experience them.

His Patience

The successful black man has done the aforementioned work on himself to arrive at a sound spiritual and emotional place in life. He is looking for the same in return when he considers a mate. Quality of life is his barometer; peace is a welcome entity in his space. A man can be patient with you and actually develop love for you; but if he does not see the results from that represent a peaceful and desirable quality of life in being with you, he will healthily choose himself. Placing blame on others for your mental state will keep you in repetitive unhealthy life cycles. Taking corrective measures to enhance your quality of life, from the inside out, translates to elevated life experiences. The choice is yours.

Self Reflection

> The mirror is one of the most powerful instruments for self-growth when utilized correctly.

The ability to analyze your own contributions to situations that didn't go the way you desired them to go shows humility, and it leads to personal evolution.

> **There is always something to be gleaned from life's unfortunate outcomes if humility is present, and self-reflection is a fixture.**

When you value someone and lose them there exists an opportunity for tremendous personal growth, when what the mirror shows you is accepted. Once it is accepted you can decide as to the type of person you will carry through life moving forward. Acceptance of what you see, and the decision to take corrective measures, ensures a more evolved version of you will move through life. This is how you use every life experience, unfortunate or fortunate, to serve you, as opposed to it taking a piece of you with it.

The Importance of Mental Health

Importance of good mental health is that you attract someone who is in a linear vein mentally, and you are calibrated to the mentally healthy man. A primary goal of mine, in writing this book, is to create a mindset that encourages healthy relationships. The better your mental health, the more likely you are to experience healthy relationships.

The successful black man has overcome and frequently encounters struggles. It was definitely a struggle to arrive at a place of consistent success, given he was not supposed to arrive there according to the power structure. His adverse consistent circumstance stems from him actually making it, and people being discontent that he arrived at a place society is not designed for him to be. He gets it coming and going.

He wants his world to be as much of a sanctuary as it possibly can. Chaos and conflict may have been a fixture on his journey to his respective mountain top, but he will eliminate anything that represents unnecessary frequent conflict from his sanctuary.

When you show up into his space as a mentally healthy version of yourself, with the effects of any trauma you may have encountered in life resolved, the successful black man will see you as an addition to his peaceful space, as peace is you at your essence.

The successful black man will not be hasty in his decision making of who he allows into his space. If you represent peace and tranquility consistently over time, you are making the decision easy for him in regard to you being a fixture in his world. He eschews conflict and unnecessary drama, so he is naturally bringing peace and tranquility into your space. The compatibility will be acknowledged and respected.

The Alignment

When you work on yourself and face the residual effects from traumas you experienced, you naturally become stable and peaceful. When you make this turn, you are now postured for a peaceful and stable mate. If you both are at one with yourselves and are whole, you'll both accept nothing less than what each other represent. As simple as this sounds, it's really that simple. Compatibility represents alignment, and it is evidence that you two see the world in a similar vein, and have corresponding values and ways of moving through life. It's not a personality; we are all perfectly unique. It's an essence.

You want to avoid going through life accumulating baggage, when the man you can build a healthy life and future with, travels very light. Develop yourself and your perception of yourself consistently, so when you do encounter the man who represents an ideal life experience with you, you two will share an undeniable compatibility. When you develop yourself to this degree it is impossible for you to engage in unhealthy situations, as you will see anything that is symptomatic of that as not being a part of your world. I've literally said these words verbatim to a woman: "This is not a part of my life." The successful black man, when encountered with consistent and unprovoked illogical behavior toward him, will speak those words as well, while hastily finding the nearest exit.

Your Source

The Source of All Creation has every solution to any problem you will ever encounter in your life's journey. Counselors and therapists are instrumental in arriving at a place of wholeness; but the All Knowing, Omniscient Creator, God, who manifested you here, has the capacity to heal every wound. You always want to incorporate your Source in your journey of healing and restoration. His supernatural hand can eradicate any residual effects of unwarranted traumatic life events. Counselors and therapists are instrumental, and they have a purpose and calling to perform their work. But, you should always go to the highest floor in the building when you have any need. God works from the inside out given that He created each of us. He doesn't have to ask questions and begin to deduce the origins of your troubles. He sees all and knows all. Understanding the gravity of your Source will make leaning to Him for healing and alignment your first course of action.

The Hierarchy

Abraham Maslow, the famous American psychologist, said that self-actualization sits atop every human need. Maslow believed having a deep oneness, awareness, and appreciation of yourself took precedence over every other human need. I subscribe to his theory in totality. Self-actualized people are clear mentally, spiritually, and emotionally, and they tend to be centered. Essentially, self-actualization facilitates a person's ability to master their life.

A person has mastered their life when they consistently have the experiences, in every area of their life, that bring them fulfillment.

I'm not painting the successful black man as a perfect creature. He simply knows himself enough to understand what type of people, being in his space, represent the fulfillment he is accustomed to. Gratification is a fixture in his life because he understands himself enough to know what brings him gratification. The appreciation he has for himself will not allow people into his world that do not bring to him what he brings to them. Unhealthy situations are foreign to him, as he does not bring them to people, and evades anything that is symptomatic of one. He is peaceful; so naturally, chaos is glaring when he encounters it.

Centered individuals are not peaceful, they are peace personified. There's an absence of regular conflict in their lives because they are genuinely fulfilled in every area of their life, making them happy. Happiness lends itself to peace.

Understand yourself enough to become so fulfilled that you exude peace. This is something you do for yourself so that it becomes who you are at your core. You can keep up a happy façade for a little while, but time and vulnerability reveal all. Becoming self-actualized is serving yourself by setting the stage for you to experience the highest quality of life, where gratification is ever present, and conflict does not exist.

> **If you are not conflicted internally, then you do not engage in conflict externally.**

Self-Awareness and Self-Respect

Being centered means that you will not engage in situations that don't match you. This is how you perpetually travel light. Anything that doesn't align with who you are and how you see the world simply does not stay in your space. A person who can potentially bring unhealthy energies to your life just doesn't make it into your threshold, eradicating their ability to make that toxic deposit into your space.

> **It's never about what is presented to you in life; rather, it's about what you allow into your space that determines your quality of life.**

Self-aware people understand this.

When you are at one with yourself, you will happen to life, and life will not happen to you.

When life happens to you, in ways that you could have controlled, residuals are always left behind, and you find yourself in a reactionary position trying to reverse the effects of toxic people. When you happen to life, you find yourself in an anticipatory position and you stop toxicity from entering your space. These parallels are concrete in nature, and you only fall on one side of the spectrum. On which side is determined by your tenacity in arriving at a place of personal clarity and wholeness.

You want to be available to the right type of man. This comes at the expense of perpetually working on yourself and consequently traveling light, as you better understand yourself as you progress through life. Once you do this you will keep a short account with nonsense, preventing the accumulation of baggage that translates into toxic behaviors and internal turmoil. Consciously becoming the best version of yourself daily, and healing from life's unfavorable ordeals, keeps you optimistic and available. Work on yourself until you are peace. Then you can be his peace.

Notes and Insights

Notes and Insights

Chapter 8

Keep It Tight

Men are visual. The initial interest that people have in one another is usually derived from physical appearance. When I see a woman that is physically in shape, it speaks to her lifestyle, and likely will translate to her remaining that way in the future. Physical fitness in a woman is great in the moment, and well into her future. It is a desirable trait that serves the woman well and is attractive on many levels to potential mates.

An associate of mine, who is in his late fifties to early sixties, explained to me one day as we discussed fitness that he and his wife engage in healthy eating, coupled with exercise. His reasoning was that, barring a catastrophic event, he does not want the responsibility of taking care of his wife due to poor health decisions. He held himself to the same standard of living, as he did not deem it fair to place that burden on his wife.

Physical appearance and health conscious living makes a man optimistic for the future with a woman due to the positive implications that play out over the coming years.

Balanced Living

Mental, spiritual, emotional, and physical wellbeing contribute to a high quality of life; and make you balanced overall. This way of living breeds contentment with and within yourself. The internal contentment within yourself and the establishment of the high quality of life on your own exudes that no man can complete you. This is appealing because the successful black man is complete in the aforementioned areas himself.

When you are complete you will be emotionally available to the right type of man. This is the man who is complete and content on his own, and completely open and available to the right type of woman. Being content and whole means that the wrong people can present themselves to you, but you do not allow them into your space.

A woman recently asked me how long I've been single. I responded with, "five years." I explained that I've met a few women since then that I've wanted to explore something long-term with, but I saw too much, and simply chose not to explore those interactions any further. She then asked me why I kept attracting these types of women. I explained to her that you cannot control who you encounter, you can only control who you let in. If you are attracted to someone physically, usually you'll engage with them further to see how compatible you two are. From there the decision to explore something further, in terms of dating and relationships, is established. I explained to this woman that I date women I have a high level of interest in exclusively, to take an unencumbered look at them to see how compatible we are.

I view compatibility as the absence of frequent conflict.

If two individuals are compatible, they are not exactly alike in personality and traits; they simply share a similar view of the world and have common values. This is how they do not engage in frequent conflict. Conflict is inevitable, as you have two human beings adjusting to one another. Frequent conflict conveys that two people are too far off in very important areas that determine the quality of that relationship.

I further explained to this young lady that I have not attracted a woman until she is my significant other, because I have then allowed her into my space. Encountering people and being interested is one thing; allowing people into your space that continuously bring you unfavorable experiences alludes to internal unresolved flaws in the person who continues to allow this.

This is the car analogy I used to crystallize what I was explaining to this particular young lady. I explained to her that my favorite automobile is Mercedes-Benz. You see all kinds of cars on the road, and you may even admire some of them. In the end, the observation of vehicles that aren't Mercedes Benz is just that: observation. Gravitation is reserved for the Mercedes-Benz because that it what I desire. Observing and moving toward something are completely different entities. One cannot be mistaken for the other. In totality, I explained to her that I figuratively observed some very attractive cars, but didn't find the characteristics that speak to the level of the Mercedes-Benz, so I have yet to make a purchase in the time I've been single.

The Quintessential Woman

When you are tight physically, spiritually, mentally, and emotionally, you are the quintessential black woman to the successful black man.

The successful black man is content and has arrived at a place in life where fulfillment in the many facets of his life is present. This man needs nothing from anyone, so whoever he allows into his space brings him fulfillment and is a healthy addition to his life. He is compatible with the woman who is complete on her own, because he is whole as well. This man can only be offered companionship. The woman he desires is whole because she has found fullness in the physical, spiritual, mental, and emotional areas of her life. To be whole in these areas reflects personal discipline and healthy awareness of oneself and the world around them. This level of wholeness is enticing and not intimidating to the successful black man. Any man who is intimidated by your completeness and fulfillment within yourself, is looking for you to be dependent on them somehow. This type of man is insecure, and that trait alone will translate to a tumultuous experience with him.

> **The successful black man needs no woman; he desires the right type of woman to be in his world.**

The right type of woman will need no man, rather desire the right type of man to be in her space. When these two people meet, and the attraction is present, real magic will occur.

Be the woman, to the man that has it all, that he simply desires to not live without when he encounters you. Different vehicles share the road daily. Be his fixation. Be his Mercedes-Benz.

The Ideal Experience

When an emphasis is placed on improving yourself in the areas this chapter focuses on, you now become the ideal experience for the successful black man. He understands that the woman who possesses the aforementioned amazing character traits will translate to the ideal experience in his life.

> **When someone is whole, they have the experiences they desire in every area of their life.**

It's amazing when a whole man encounters a whole woman that he desires. Nothing but anticipation will surround you in his eyes, because he understands that his existing amazing experience is about to be catapulted to a dimension he has yet to experience.

Notes and Insights

Notes and Insights

Chapter 9
Despise Opportunistic Behavior

How To Be Appealing To Successful Black Men... For Black Women

The successful black man values his financial resources and will retreat if you are a threat to him maintaining these resources. He is accustomed to women, of all social classes, approaching him as if they are the prize, and the financial red carpet must be laid out in order to grace their presence. He is no stranger to opportunistic behavior from women, as they size him up and make attempts to extort resources from him.

Opportunistic behavior is detestable on many levels; but it's the disrespect of telling a successful black man that you are so much more valuable than him that he has to make a financial exchange to be in your presence that is the most glaring.

Successful black men adore black women, as proven in the statistic that 85 percent of married black men making over six figures are married to black women. That's essentially nine out of ten, which is implicit of a reverence, allegiance to, and desire for black women.

With 72 percent of black women forecasted to never be married in their lifetime, and a statistical fact that successful black men are marrying black women, opportunistic behavior toward a successful black man makes no sense at all.

If your desire is to ultimately partner with a successful black man, an opportunistic thought should never enter your mind while in his presence. If your desire is to elevate yourself and your status solely by entertaining the black man, it would make sense to extract whatever resources you can. But to desire a healthy and lasting union with a successful black man, give him the peace of mind that you are showing up to get to know him, and not his wallet.

Prize Thinking

The "I am the prize" mindset is what fuels opportunistic behavior toward men. The successful black man can easily deduce the quality of woman who stands before him very quickly. The real conversation is the one that doesn't physically take place. If you are a prize, then that will reveal itself without having to be promoted or articulated to him.

If we are talking leverage in the dating game, the amount of successful black men, in comparison to successful black women, is lopsided to say the least. The successful black man would never lord this societal leverage over any woman he meets, due to his security within himself. He's aware for sure; but identifying with and using disparity of successful black women to successful black men to manipulate a situation is not in his nature. He would never approach you as if he is the prize. He will approach you eye to eye, with the hope that you view him as an equal as well.

The successful black man subscribes to the biblical offering, "He who findeth a wife, findeth a good thing." The woman who embodies the characteristics, mannerisms, and essence of the "good thing" the biblical offering speaks of will be acknowledged as so. She will be revered as his prize, and not the prize.

Lopsided Dynamics

Any rational and intelligent man can look around at the plethora of unhealthy relationships and marriages around him, and understand that the men who subscribe to the women in their life as being "the prize," experience a lifetime of always having to cater to the never ending demands of their significant other. This relationship dynamic is as toxic as they come, and it will subject him to a life of disrespect from his significant other.

> **The dynamic that is established in the beginning of the interaction is the one that pervades the duration of the relationship.**

With this being the reality, presenting yourself as the prize to the successful black man is an assured way to no longer be in his space, as you do not view him the way he views himself. It's a miserable life to always be the one carrying the relationship and endlessly catering to a woman. This type of man exists in large numbers, but you will not respect him as a man. You will always desire the solid man who respects himself, and you'll be vulnerable to this man if you partner with someone who doesn't respect themselves. You can't respect a man who you walk all over. The masculine man who respects himself, must be approached at eye level, as he understands how initial interaction dynamics set the stage for the rest of the relationship.

Financial Footing

The successful black man values the woman who is stable financially or is consistently working toward her own financial independence.

It's a highly attractive trait for a woman to enjoy the rewards of being with a successful black man, while still being able to provide whatever lifestyle she'd like to experience on her own.

If you have strong financial footing, and do not require him to financially lavish you upon first meeting, he will begin to see you through a long term vantage, as you make him feel safe that his finances will not be compromised. You will be a departure from his consistent experience of women attempting to angle their way into his wallet.

Caught Up In The Matrix

In my newly released book, "The Successful Dreamer: How To Unapologetically Live Your Truth," I have an entire chapter devoted to escaping the matrix. The matrix is systematic control based on the population being driven by valuing themselves based on meaningless material possessions. The matrix is a perpetual dangling carrot. Just when you thought you've acquired the necessary material possession to validate you as "exclusive" in societal posturing, something else comes along that is more exclusive. This cycle never ends, with the design being to always keep the consumer in financial distress, no matter how much money they make. The more money a person has, the less they can be controlled. Significant amounts of money give freedom and options that are not afforded to you when your material possessions and debt wake you up every morning, and make you do things you do not desire to do, but have to do. This is the matrix.

The successful black man is vigilant enough to see the matrix for what it is. When a woman requires financially extravagant treatment as soon as they meet, it's telling. He concludes that she doesn't have financial wherewithal, and that she's constantly validating herself through material acquisition as social proof that she is so "exclusive," with hundreds of thousands of dollars in debt hanging over her head. He understands that the requirement of him to have to provide upscale experiences for you is indicative of your attitude toward money and material validation. He understands that in your mind you associate the dispensation of finances on you equates to how much a person values you. Not the intangibles such as time, devotion, dedication, and kind gestures validating the level of the man's interest in you; but how much of his resources he's willing to part with so you can tell your girlfriends how this man is lavishing you, so you appear, in that moment, superior in your circle of women who possess financially detrimental mindsets.

The successful and financially conscious black man wants no part of that. He either has no debt, or he is aggressively attacking his debt. He desires freedom, not the bondage that terrible financial footing creates. If your first course of action, when entering his space, is to take advantage of him financially, he will see you as a detriment to his financially free reality, which has created the lifestyle he has and wants to experience for the rest of his life. He will easily choose his lifestyle over you.

If you arrive in this man's space with solid financial footing and the mindset to remain in a favorable financial place, due to your healthy attitude toward money and the material world, you will be a welcome addition to his space. If your validation is in material possessions and the appearance of success you will be deemed as incompatible with the man whose identity is within himself, and not in the validation of material acquisitions. If the attempt to engage in opportunistic behavior is your first course of action with the successful black man, he will easily see that you are not postured to his way of moving financially, and that you represent avoidable conflict.

Setting The Stage

Imagine this scenario. A man asks you out to dinner. Of course, it is implicit that he should pay given he has no clue of your financial situation, and should operate within financial boundaries of the evening he requested your presence to partake in. You two have great food and conversation. The bill comes and you say listen, this ones on me; or you say we're still getting to know each other, so let's take care of our own bill tonight. He's rarely heard anything remotely close to this. You would blow his mind, especially if you are the highly desirable, tight woman I spoke of in the previous chapter. He would understand, in an instant, that this could actually be something.

What you must understand as a woman is that there are things that you can do that are such as departure from the frequent off putting behavior the successful black man encounters, that he will be sold on you as someone he knows he'd like to be with, and work backwards with you over time to see the level of compatibility you two share. He will literally be so into you that he desires you on enough levels that he would be satisfied if you were the last woman he ever had to date, and move forward with you by actually moving backwards because he's already mentally and spiritually arrived at the end with you; but he understands the importance of compatibility, and his eye is fixated on determining that. Understand the power of captivating a man. This is a different experience. He is captivated because you are a physical and spiritual embodiment of everything he has ever desired. You are a departure from his consistent experience with women. He will easily conclude that he can park in whatever space you two occupy. The end is established. Working backward will determine if you two can do it for a lifetime.

When I speak of working backward because he sees you as his future, this is the ideal position to be in with a successful black man. He desires you on such an intense level, due to what he's seen in you, that he begins to detach from any other women he is involved with. He meets new women, and it's as if he is going through the motions no matter how attractive these women are. He is fixated on you at this point and satisfied enough with what he's seen in you and the feelings that are intensifying by the second for you. You are his fixation, but you are not his final destination. The final destination is when he's seen you over time and understands that his experience with you will be ideal for a lifetime. The beautiful part is that being his fixation is the predecessor to being his final destination.

When you are his quintessential woman, he will speak to you from places he rarely, if ever, speaks to women from. He will effortlessly speak to you from his soul. There will be no hesitation, only acknowledgement on his part that this extremely unordinary woman inspires me to speak to her from unchartered internal depths. I promise you. When he begins to speak to you from this place, he is yours to lose. Show him a healthy version of yourself over a period of time after he arrives at this place, and you may as well prepare your wedding registry. He will be completely gone with you and see his optimal future experience with you by is side.

Inspire vs. Require

Requiring a successful black man to lavish you financially without even knowing you is a way of moving that is vastly perpetuated by mainstream female rappers as well as reality television, and other mediums of black media images. A woman requiring a man to greet her with finances represents a non-elevated consciousness and low-level thinker. The successful black man, being the intuitive and cerebral man that he is, will immediately view you, and this behavior, as a headache that will quickly and frequently manifest itself. This thought process and behavior by women is low vibration that conflicts with the successful black man's high frequency. A financially savvy and prosperous man has arrived at this place by being intelligent with his money. The easiest way to turn him off is to require him to spend his hard-earned money lavishly on you to be in the presence of such a "prize." It's easy to see that his free way of living, due to intelligent financial decisions, would be compromised quickly by allowing you and your entitled mindset into his space. He will choose himself and his lifestyle over you easily and exit your space in the most expeditious manner.

Entitled thinking and requests only work on low value men who, essentially, do not value themselves. If a man does not value himself and cannot reach a place of oneness within himself, he is unstable in many ways, and will set the stage for a tumultuous life if you partner with him. Instability will be a fixture in your life because the only way either one of you could remain in the other's space is to operate on a similar frequency, which represents the compatibility you two share.

The successful black man, when inspired, looks forward to lavishing the woman in his life with the best of everything. This woman will be the one who displayed elevated thinking and did not require him to go headfirst with his wallet to engage in an interaction with her. If he is into you, and sees that you are into him the same way, without the material world playing a part in the interaction you two share, he will gladly do nice things for you; simply because you inspired him to do so, with no inclination of entitlement in the equation.

In Real Time

A few years back one of my good friends and I hadn't gotten together in months. We decided to meet up at an after-work spot in Washington, D.C. I was still dressed in my tailored Italian suit, with high end decorative elements. My friend and I were just hanging out when a young lady stopped and looked at me. I wasn't in the mindset to interact with any women that day. Catching up with my friend would suffice for that evening.

The young lady made her friends wait as she looked at me; my friend and I both knew that she wasn't going anywhere until I said something to her. The young lady and I met and exchanged numbers. We texted a little back and forth over the next couple of days and decided to meet up. I picked a very nice restaurant with a Sunday happy hour. I was very clear that we were meeting up to have beverages and converse. I could already see the play taking shape before we met up. She was slow on the responses to my messages except when it came to meeting up. She was lining me up for the #foodiecall.

We arrived at the restaurant and met by the bar which had the section where the happy hour was taking place. We exchanged pleasantries and began to converse. She explained that she had just moved to D.C., and that she was furnishing her apartment and looking for a bed. I explained to her that I had recently helped someone find a memory foam mattress very inexpensively, and that Groupon and Wayfair were viable cost-efficient options for home goods.

Right then she could see that although I was the image of prosperity when we initially met, I wasn't loose with my money. She then went onto to give her prepared speech on how she had been drinking all weekend, and how she had wrapped up a brunch earlier with her friends that was full of mimosas. The soliloquy continued with her saying that she was health conscious, and that she had been meal prepping and wanted to stay away from the drinks. She then proceeded to ask the bartender for a regular food menu, bypassing the bar menu. She then proceeded to order the most expensive item on the menu. Her energy was that of she was enduring the conversation and was there for the food. Her food came very quickly, and she excused herself to the bathroom, placing a napkin over her food.

She returned from the bathroom and I shot it straight. I explained that we were meeting for drinks, and that I would cover my drink. Based on her deducing that I had money, but was financially intelligent, resulting from our bedding conversation, she said: "I'd figure you would do that." She still tried me though because she likely knew every intricate detail of the menu hours before our arrival, and she developed her game plan accordingly. I knew what was coming next. She said she was okay with it, even though the energy completely changed. Forty-five seconds later, she said to me: "No man has ever done that to me; I'd like to eat my food alone." I found the bartender and covered my beverage and gladly departed.

She attempted to shame me given I wouldn't allow her to take advantage of me. In reality, her attempt had nothing to do with me, because I established a boundary that was violated. This is what the successful black man regularly encounters. Will you be the departure from this type of opportunistic behavior and let him know that your interest lies in him and not his financial means? The successful black man would never engage in this type of behavior with you and will not accept it toward him.

A woman of elevated consciousness and thinking would never move in the aforementioned manner with any man. Understand that the successful black man values himself and will eschew any behavior toward him that doesn't align with how he sees himself. When you show up as the elevated best version of yourself, you will naturally inspire the man you are involved with to lavish you, with no coercion.

The successful black man goes through life understanding that he is enough. The person he has become, and continues to evolve into, is enough for any person, let alone any woman. There exists no place within him that will acquiesce to a woman's irrational demands to lavish her to be in her presence. He will literally laugh at the notion. He in no way leads in with his wallet; he leads in with his essence. In the above story, when I met the young woman, I never mentioned that I was an author who just came from a book signing. I believe men leading in with their accomplishments and decorations exude a low frequency type of energy. It signals to any woman that you are insecure and primed to be taken advantage of, given you are not at one with yourself, and have so much to prove to the world around you. That man is tailored to be taken for a ride.

Always seek out the man who is secure within himself, as no circumstance or situation can knock this man off of his equilibrium. He is centered. He understands himself, and will provide you with stability, which transcends the benefits of meaningless material possessions. The only constant in the material world is change. If a man leads in with what he can do for you, his identity is in the material world. Everything in the material world is non-substantive and fleeting. The man who identifies with the material world above all is unstable in all of his ways. The man who is secure within himself, regardless of where he sits in the pecking order of societal standing, has a God consciousness. His identity is whatever God says about him, and not in the expectations and requirements that must be in place for society to celebrate you. God says that He is the same yesterday, today, and forever more. Which man would you like to appeal to? Which man will you be postured to, to exist in his world? Your choice is a relationship of instability, or a relationship anchored in the only stability that exists.

Notes and Insights

Notes and Insights

Chapter 10
It's Too Good to Be True

You may desire the quintessential man who checks all of your boxes. The man that you've prayed for may manifest, but will you be ready to receive him?

You may not be in a prominent place according to society's standards, but the man across from you is. Do not falter to the opinions of insecure people who don't believe this man will want anything lasting with you. Negative opinions come from insecurity and jealousy. I've seen this play out firsthand with a young lady I was over the top interested in, who had the entire world going for her. Here is my recount.

I met a gorgeous young lady who was arguably one of the most beautiful creations I ever laid eyes on. We immediately hit it off from the moment we met. We shared commonalities in our beliefs and had very similar outlooks on things that we were valuable to us as individuals. We were compatible on many levels. The attraction and spark we shared was tangible; it was visible and ever present. People would just smile at us. We inspired people. I saw happiness in random, older white women when we were together. I saw hope in the eyes of some of the young black women who saw us. Unconsciously and effortlessly, I always let my sentiment of adoration toward this woman show when we were together. It was genuine and true, and could not be denied. I wanted her to have the best experience possible when we were together, and for her to never question my level of anticipation of what I'd hope we'd become. I was all in.

This young lady, outside of the many degrees she possessed and was working toward, had a beauty so rare that people looked at her as if time stopped. God dealt her one of the most favorable hands I've ever seen a woman close to me possess. Every fiber of my being hoped that she was my final destination in life, as I easily let go of any other woman I was involved with, to take an unencumbered look at her to determine our level of compatibility. I was literally working backward, as I stated previously, because what I saw initially enraptured me. I was hers to lose.

This young lady told her mother about me. She was extremely excited to let the people closest to her know that I was in her life. Her mother said, right on cue, "Why would a man in that position want to be with you?" Her daughter possessed an abundance of desirable traits and characteristics, and those were her mother's words to her. She then told her classmates, who were all attending a prestigious university in Washington, D.C., and they echoed her mother's sentiment toward my presence in her life, verbatim. It came out later in our interaction that her brother shared the popular opinion of me being too successful to want to deal with someone who was extremely decorated, but still finding her way in life.

The young lady did not have a perception of herself that aligned with the incredible hand that God dealt her. That set the stage for all of those opinions to fester and create a story in her mind that I was too good to be true. Her actions were in accordance with those opinions as time progressed, with her admitting that she never believed that I wanted to be with her, despite my unwavering presence and actions that proved otherwise.

I was patient, but ultimately had to make a quality of life decision. She presented a version of herself that aligned with the belief that this is too good to be true. The atmosphere was toxic. I made a decision that I in no way wanted to make, as I had real feelings for this woman. It was a decision I had to make, as the compatibility just wasn't there. I had to take a hard look at my quality of life before she entered my life. I chose peace.

Till this day I believe she is a wonderful woman; and I hope she is evolving and experiencing that best that God has for her.

Of the many things that ended our time together, her admission that she bought into the opinions of everyone around her concerning our probability of making it, is what cemented our fate.

Entering or Staying

God can hand deliver everything you've ever prayed for and desired into your space, but whether or not you are the person that is postured to receive this blessing, will determine if this delivery is yours to keep or will falter. Your perception of yourself will determine what stays and goes in your life. In the above story, if the young lady had seen herself as a viable match for me, the words relayed from others that were contrary to that would have not had the power to influence her consciousness and thinking.

> **When you take personal responsibility for developing a healthy perception of yourself, your entire life will come into a healthy balance. Words contrary to what you know and believe about yourself will have no weight, as you consistently become and possess everything that God has for you.**

Your life will change forever when you understand that the power is not in what is presented to you; rather, in what you allow in. Everything that attempts to enter your space will be put into its proper perspective when you revere and value yourself. Toxicity will be repelled, with all things healthy occupying a welcomed space in your world, because that is what you are calibrated to.

The Origins of Jealousy

Negative opinions typically originate from insecurity and jealousy.

If people can not see an optimal experience for themselves, it is difficult to desire optimal experiences for others. People inevitably see you through the lens they see the world with every day.

There is power in thinking in layers and identifying where the jealousy originates. Thinking in layers can be understanding that whatever stands in front of you is greater than anything that people are persuading you is not for you; it is greater than anything they have yet to experience for themselves. This is layered thinking. The origins and motive are never too far away from the jealousy.

The Worst Type of Jealousy

The worst type of jealousy is when someone looks at you and concludes that they can never have what you have. This jealousy often translates to vitriol. When you see this type of jealousy being exuded, run. Distance yourself. This is the type of jealousy that brews toxicity. I will discuss this further in the chapter, "Decided Advantages."

When layered thinking becomes a part of your natural thought process, many things around you will easily be exposed concerning people and their motives.

Emotional Intelligence

Emotional intelligence is when you understand the motive and reasoning behind the emotion that is being relayed to you. Jealousy is an emotion. When it is expressed it usually is not effective in its design to derail you from whatever blessing you are experiencing, if you know the origin and motive of it. Jealousy is often expressed in a manipulative way to get you to not be able to partake of the blessings that your makeup and characteristics suggest you are qualified for.

Emotional intelligence, when developed and applied, allows you to actually turn your lens back to you and celebrate the very things that people are attempting to rob you of the experience of partaking in. It makes you acknowledge the wonderful characteristics, talents, and attributes that intimidate people to the point they try to manipulate you out of your blessings by trying to get you to doubt yourself.

Many people do not possess the presence of mind and belief in themselves to be the match for the wonderful blessings that life has in store for them. Consequently, they encounter the blessings, but they slip through their fingers because they are not a calibrated landing space for the blessings. Take a hard look at the person's life who tries to downplay your qualification for the blessings that are attempting to enter your space. You will see clearly and quickly that nothing currently in their life is on the level of what your potential affords to you; that's where their jealousy for you exists. Do not get mad, and develop an "I'll show you!" attitude toward the individual(s) relaying their jealousy of you to you;

instead, simply make the observation and place your energy and intention on the blessings that are in your space, so you can possess them and experience their fullness.

The Timing of the Jealousy

True colors are rarely shown until the threat of you realizing your potential becomes real.

In the story told in this chapter, the manipulation, entrenched in jealousy, was not implemented until a man entered her daughter's life that was in line with the woman her daughter had become. Her daughter had accomplished some thing in life, and had some things going for her that she would never get to experience. The moment that the blessing entered her daughter's life, that was in line with the woman that she had become, and all of the potential was becoming reality, the vitriol was unleashed. Young black women, if you do not learn to decipher everything that surrounds the jealousy that is spewed at you, the intent behind the jealousy will overtake you.

When you move up the ladder of success, and your potential in major areas of your life is becoming reality, be on the lookout for attempts to thwart you from experiencing the fullness of everything you attract from the woman that you've evolved into. You deserve every positive blessing that will present itself to you. Develop an impeccable opinion of yourself so your first course of action is to receive the blessing, with no thought given to the tactics of detractors, and no hesitation being present in your step toward your blessings.

In my life, it was one thing to tell people I was going to become an author and motivational speaker when I was in college. But to graduate with a book contract at 22 years old brought about the reality of the potential that I possessed. When my books were being written and published is when I saw the most vicious attacks undertaken against me, all to discourage me from operating in and experiencing the blessings that would elevate me past people, in their minds.

If you respect and observe the timing of it all, it will make sense. It will also enlighten you to the low energy tactics deployed against you. Most importantly, it will open your eyes to the realization of your potential, as people around you tremor in the face of you becoming everything that they know you are designed to be.

Do Better

There may be some older black women reading this book. Please do not attempt to thwart the growth and blessings of the younger women you encounter who have amazing things going for themselves. Be the woman you wish you had been when you were their age that could have catapulted you further in life, had you encountered the elevated wisdom to take you there. You have enough life experience to relay jewels to these young women that will elevate them to levels you never experienced. There are some opportunities that these young women have that have escaped you. Deliver your gift of experience to these young women, with a heart to see them surpass you, and not vitriol toward them for doing so. Leave the young black woman, who enters your space, better. You will be rewarded for it. The All-Knowing Omniscient Creator knows and sees all.

Young women, time stops for no one, and by God's grace you will be the elder full of wisdom one day. Please be the woman for the young women that you desired when you were their age. Even the girls who are slightly younger than you; you have some experiences they haven't had. Pay the wisdom forward and be the blessing you desire to experience.

Accept the Delivery

Labeling something as too good to be true is saying that God is not capable of delivering what you prayed for.

If God brings certain things and people into your life, then He sees you as deserving of whatever He is depositing into your atmosphere. Until you accept and understand how God sees you, you will always not see yourself as worthy of whatever He bestows upon you. You will encounter great people and opportunities but will miss out on the ability to experience the fullness of the potential experience, because you will sabotage it due to feelings of ineptness.

If you go through life with a God consciousness, the efforts of man to dissuade you from seeing yourself as deserving of amazing life experiences will be void of power and impact in your life. Imagine if someone said the words to you: "You are not worthy of this great man who stands before you," and your first thought was "I am fearfully and wonderfully made." When you have a God consciousness, everything is placed into perspective that enters your space. You will grasp every blessing because you see yourself in the brightest possible light: in the image of your Creator, worthy of everything He has for you.

A God consciousness is necessary in a world of insecure and competitive people. The powers understand how powerful people would be if they saw themselves in a healthy light and with value. This is the matrix I speak of. It exists to control and manipulate people into submission to forward the self-serving agendas of the elite. We are not encouraged to value ourselves. We are too dangerous if we do so. A people who value themselves without wavering would be true to their own callings and destinies, so defining your value by societal benchmarks, material acquisitions, and the opinions of others will be a staple as long as the earth remains.

Many people will feel threatened when you potentially have something more valuable than them because society says your value is contingent upon being more prosperous, and existing on higher footing than the people around you. You should almost expect that the jealousy will spew when the reality of actualizing your potential presents itself. It's natural for women to immediately tell you that you are not worthy of an incredible man, when he enters your presence, because they have yet to capture the man on the level that they desire. It's societal conditioning. If your consciousness is not on the opinion that your Creator has of you, the web of conformity will encapsulate you, with not exceeding the accomplishments of those who surround you.

The Confidence to Receive

The confidence to receive every blessing that life has for you comes in two ways, while equating to having the optimal perception of yourself. The first way is God consciousness. Understanding what God says about you and His perception of you as being worthy, makes you receptive to any blessing that enters your space. You spiritually match whatever is presented to you, and you consequently receive it and experience the fullness of it. When this is your first line of thought, you will boldly and confidently accept the incredible man that is for you, as well as the many blessings and great experiences that will befall you.

The second way to be confident enough to receive any blessing that is presented to you is to become the best version of yourself in every given moment and season of your life. If you look at the story in this chapter, the young lady and I were in different seasons in life, with me experiencing the prosperity of my efforts, and her diligently undertaking the measures necessary to actualize her life's vision. Our seasons were different; but our movements were similar, given that we both weren't satisfied, understood there was more to be accomplished, and took the daily necessary steps to arrive at whatever "there" represented to us as individuals.

You can stand in confidence in the reality that you are not standing around waiting on life to happen to you; you are imposing your will on life daily toward your goals, and impacting the outcomes you desire to experience at their optimal levels. This is where you can place your confidence to receive anything that enters your space. Do not worry about whatever season you are in; find confidence and solace that you are fervently influencing your desired life outcomes, daily. You will arrive at a favorable destination. Never allow society to influence the value of that destination. If the destination is true to you and brings you fulfillment, your highest gratification is in this place.

You ultimately want to develop yourself, and the perception you have of yourself, so it aligns with the great things that life is going to bestow upon you. There will always be a myriad of detractors and jealous individuals who attempt to sabotage the blessings that your potential warrants. Develop your mind and spirit to the point that when this vitriol is presented to you, you simply reply with: "That has nothing to do with me," as you capture every blessing that befalls you.

You are gifted. You are brilliant. You are great. You are worthy. Believe.

Notes and Insights

Notes and Insights

Chapter 11

The Defense Rests

Life will take away from you or you will take away from life. An easy and efficient way to run off a man is to always be on the defensive. A life of drama and unnecessarily difficult situations is created from letting life get the best of you, and choosing to not evolve from all experiences, good and bad. Life is nothing more than a series of glorified recurrences; it's the same situations happening repeatedly. Your quality of life depends on how you evolve from situation to situation, not allowing life's inevitable turmoil to take valuable pieces of yourself away every time you endure unfavorable circumstances.

> **Personal growth is a different response to the same situation.**

Your growth determines how enjoyable your life will be as you progress through it. Every life circumstance, favorable or unfavorable, has the power to serve you by using the wisdom from the experience to become a more evolved and conscious version of yourself. This is how you take away from life, and not have life take away from you.

Choose To Learn

I've been in relationships where I knew I was the culprit for things ending, and I've been in relationships that I was completely wronged. Instead of resorting to shame for my misgivings in the relationship or accumulating baggage and bashing the individual who wronged me, I simply chose to learn from every situation. This knowledge translated to me evolving and understanding myself better and what personality types and traits that I am compatible with. I learned anything from how to treat women better in my life and acknowledge characteristics that make a woman special, to understanding the importance of women possessing mental strength and not being able to be easily influenced by people around her. This knowledge came packaged in circumstances where I was wrong and had been wronged, but I chose to focus on the greatest gift that existed when it was over: the opportunity to learn and grow from the experience.

Devastation, blame, pain, and regret are ever present entities when a relationship or prolonged interaction comes to an end. You are human so you have to experience these emotions and decompress the situation when it culminates, as this is healthy and normal.

After you process the emotions you have to make a concrete decision to not allow the situation to get the best of you.

> **Personal evolution is not a given, it is a choice. Knowledge is an invaluable gift that continues to serve you as long as you consistently apply it.**

After the emotions subside, there exists the opportunity to take a better and more evolved version of yourself through life, and in interactions you will have with men moving forward.

Years ago, a relationship that I was involved in came to an end. It was one of those "why in the world did I stay in it as long as I did" relationships. I was hurt and devastated, with my overarching sentiment being that I never wanted to experience anything like that again in my life.

One day, shortly after my breakup, I was randomly flipping through television channels. I came across Pastor Joel Osteen preaching a message on letting go. He gave examples of two individuals from his congregation that had been wronged in marriages, and he exposed the devastating effects of not healing and moving on. Pastor Osteen also exposed the glorious results of healing from traumatic experiences and finding a more balanced and healthy love.

The first lady who Pastor Osteen spoke of was cheated on and left by her husband. She replayed her ex-husband's actions in her mind like a recurring movie, and the reality of what he did to her festered deeply, creating the unhealthiest of baggage moving forward. This woman eventually met a good man in the church who treated her right and conducted himself in an upright manner, being the polar opposite of the husband who left her. She repeatedly made the new man pay for the sins of her ex-husband. The man was patient and gave the relationship time to see if her trauma could be resolved, but the toxicity from her only magnified over time. The man chose himself, understanding that he was receiving underserved treatment from this new woman in his life, and valued himself enough to leave the situation.

Pastor Osteen agreed with how the man handled the situation and stood behind him for leaving the woman. He simply didn't deserve the treatment he was receiving, so he had every right to choose himself in that situation.

Pastor Osteen then went on to tell the story of a great man in his congregation who loved his wife endlessly and believed his marriage was void of any visible or underlying problems. This man's wife left the marriage with a note to him that only expressed that she was leaving. To make it worse, his ex-wife left no explanation whatsoever to explain her reasoning behind her rash decision. This man loved his wife with all of his heart, and experienced unthinkable devastation. He sought council from Pastor Osteen, with the pastor admonishing the gentlemen to take healthy measures to heal and move on with his life.

One day after service, the gentlemen found Pastor Osteen, and with a renewed and bright countenance told the pastor that he had found a new love, and he didn't know such a deep love existed. He loved this new woman from a depth he didn't know he possessed.

Pastor Osteen said that since this man went through his grief and healed, he was open to receive the blessings that were coming his way. Pastor Osteen said, "God will give you beauty for your ashes."

Pastor Osteen then went on to say that it's natural to mourn a loss in your life, but there comes a time that if you don't let it go the effects of the traumatic event, it will harm you moving forward in life. He admonished his audience to let go of any hurtful and devastating experiences and understand the consequences and blessings that await your decision.

God will give you beauty for your ashes when He knows you won't turn beauty into ashes.

Right after Joel Osteen went off of the air, I was flipping through channels again and came across a pastor, that I had never seen or heard before, preaching. This gentleman was a local pastor from Prince George's County, MD. He was preaching about how people have wronged you and these people have forgot about it and moved on with their life, while you are hurting yourself by holding on to the weight of the transgression against you. He was more animated than Pastor Osteen, as many of the local pastors have an inner entertainer in them, but the message was the exact same.

There was no coincidence whatsoever in the existence and synchronicity of these messages I encountered, at a time in my life where I was still facing the effects of devastation following my recently ended relationship.

Choices

Growing up my father would tell me frequently the words of our pastor, John A. Cherry, "Choices are long-lasting and life-changing." When I observed the timing of the consecutive messages I received that day, I understood that God was putting a choice before me, and showing the effects whatever choice I made regarding moving on from my former relationship. I chose to let go.

Superpowers

I made a choice to learn from the relationship and extract the jewel of wisdom that hovered in front of me. I was more thankful than hurt. Over time, when I saw how my consciousness toward women and relationships had expanded, I had an entirely new set of eyes that I viewed women and relationships through.

This relationship was short in duration, but it possessed an innumerable amount of variables that were present in its short existence. I became aware of there being no surprises in relationships, given people typically become more of what they initially show you. I understood the importance of calling black, black and blue, blue. In addition to that, I now understood that a woman can not control her family dynamics and influences, but she can control the type of woman that she is internally to not be persuaded by perspectives that do not align with the reality of the man in front of her. This was powerful, given I had no awareness of dynamics like these before I was in that relationship. When the pain subsided and I began extract the wisdom jewels, my overarching sentiment was one of thankfulness. This young lady was a gift. Not the traditional gift in the sense of relationships; but a gift, nonetheless.

She was the type of gift that continues to give until this day. I have met women after her that exuded similar characteristics and knew how the story would end if I remained in the situation. This experience has kept me in a peaceful place, living a peaceful life, by and large, since it ended. I've engaged in no unhealthy relationships since the relationship ended, and I've learned to merge patience with reality when dealing with women. I'm very happy with the man I have become, and the favorable results I've experienced in life from such an unfavorable relationship. Beauty undoubtedly emerged from the ashes. Wisdom is the principle thing.

Trust Yourself

It's easy to feel as if men, or people, are trying to get over on you, without even knowing them. This is a valid assertion given the selfish and self-serving nature of many people.

> **If you train your instincts, by taking away from experiences life has given you, you'll trust that very few things will get past you.**

This will put you in a healthy and relaxed state when dealing with people, allowing you to enjoy the person in front of you with no filter; or dismiss yourself from a situation that you can concretely see won't be healthy.

When you trust yourself, it is impossible for you to go through life in a defensive state because you trust your instincts and the cumulative wisdom you gained from prior experiences. This mindset allows you to fully engage with and experience the person who is in front of you without barriers. You want to have a pure lens to have a pure experience with people. Doing the necessary work to develop your perception of people to this point means that clarity is your ally, with a distorted lens not being a part of your being.

The Best Version of You

> Experiences are life giving you ingredients to become the best version of yourself. What you do with them determines what version of yourself you become.

If you move with the cadence of extracting applicable wisdom from every life experience, you will always be at your best and continually better your best.

Life experiences are providing you with the opportunity to develop a heightened appreciation and awareness of yourself. Once you utilize this opportunity to your advantage, the terms of your life change, given you now have the personal clarity to understand yourself enough to not allow anything or anyone into your space that is not aligned with the revelations you gained concerning yourself through life experiences. Experiences are powerful beyond measure and must be respected accordingly. The terms of engagement for your life change drastically when you accept and apply what life is showing you concerning who you are. You master your life when everything enters your space on your terms. There's no imbalance in this space; only fulfillment as you exclusively accept what brings you optimal enjoyment.

Travel Light

The successful black man is coming to you, having dealt with the inevitable unfortunate situations of life in a healthy way. He's evolved through his experiences and comes to you very light on his feet due to the absence of baggage.

If you have taken away from life, and not allowed your life circumstances to get the better of you, your lack of luggage will be visible as well. This sets the stage for a very healthy interaction, with you two entering each other's space with the effects of becoming the best version of yourself.

Please do not think I am implying perfection throughout this book. I am relaying the benefits of continually having a mindset to improve yourself, and the power of the dynamics that will be established in your life subsequently, with the stage being set for a healthy interaction with the black man you desire.

> **A conscious and consistent effort to develop yourself and find the jewel in every experience will yield undeniable positive results in your life and in your relationships.**

There's no escaping this.

Only So Many Types of People

There are only so many types of people you will encounter. The power in any previously unfavorable interaction is in developing your instincts to be able to decipher the type of person who is currently standing in front of you. There are very few surprises when it comes to people as well.

> **Character has precursors and behaviors that are indicative of the character.**

It feels great to observe behaviors in a person and be able to associate them with behaviors in people you encountered that led to outcomes you wish to not recreate. It's a luxury to have dealt with and interacted with the men you previously have. When you begin to keep a short account with individuals who share the character traits and behaviors that people you had unfavorable outcomes with exhibit, the luxury of the unfavorable prior experience is revealed. There are many ways that dealing with people can serve you. Allow the accumulation of knowledge concerning character traits and behaviors to be one of them.

If you keep having the same undesirable experiences and outcomes with men, you must observe your failure to grow and learn from each situation. There's a saying that success leaves clues. The corollary to this is: failure leaves clues as well. If you are perpetually hurt by the same type of man exhibiting the same course of action against you, the beginning of your growth is in the acceptance that you are the common denominator.

> **There must be an urgency to grow from each life situation by learning more about people and human nature, as well as yourself.**

Accept Responsibility

When you accept responsibility for developing your eye, as well as your instincts, in regard to deciphering who is in front of you, you will dismiss a defensive approach to dealing with men, and trust yourself enough to allow the man in front of you to reveal who he is, with no internal interferences from you influenced by prior unfavorable experiences.

> **No one deserves to pay for transgressions against you they haven't committed.**

You want to attract and keep the right men in your life. Giving him a clean slate, as he is mentally and emotionally well enough to do the same for you, sets the stage for a healthy interaction.

Your developed eye and impeccable instincts will place you in a relaxed state, as you are vigilant and not on the defensive constantly waiting for the other shoe to drop when dealing with men. It is attractive to the successful black man when your stance toward him is open and intelligent. Your openness reflects the trust you have for your instincts which have been developed over time. Your intelligence will be acknowledged, as it is evident that you analyze what you see against your prior experiences, and not dilute what you see through a foggy lens. If you interact with a man, and you two are both developed to this degree in dealing with the opposite gender, a present and enjoyable experience will exist, no matter the duration of the interaction.

Be Appealing

Unfortunate life circumstances and failed relationships are as standard as breathing if you experience enough life. What is appealing to an emotionally available and mentally healthy man is if you have emerged from the ashes with a beautiful radiance. It is a testament to the character traits you have acquired through choosing to evolve and not regress emotionally from devastating circumstances. This level of emotional maturity will captivate the man who shares your level of personal evolution. When you can express to a man what you have been through, and articulate the priceless life lessons you acquired as a result, and the evolved person you became by having a developed eye to never experience those controllable circumstances again, he will respect you as a layered thinker.

Moving past emotion and arriving at a place of decompressing all life situations is evidence that you are an elevated thinker.

When everything doesn't have to be pointed out to you, and you police your own evolution, by taking personal responsibility for the experiences you have in life, you exhibit long term qualities the successful black man will clamor for.

The defense rests.

Notes and Insights

Notes and Insights

Chapter 12

The Power To Change

No definition of you is concrete if you embrace your power to change.

A woman entered my life who was the purest soul I've ever experienced in my space. She loved me, unconditionally, and was all about me with no games or difficulties. I was with her for three years, and flat out mishandled her. I was a good, reliable, and present man to her in many ways; but I failed her in other facets of what a healthy relationship consists of. This woman was gift.

After the relationship ended, I chose to face myself, and the many ways that I failed this woman. It was the equivalent of the life review that people experience when they go to heaven and come back. I literally saw scenes play back from our relationship, with me seeing them from her perspective. I lost it. I couldn't believe that I conducted myself in the manner I did for such a prolonged period of time to someone who was so undeserving. When I looked at the many ways I had been less than adequate to this woman who was nothing but loving, caring, forgiving, and patient with me, it was one of the hardest moments I ever had to face in my life.

After doing so, I chose to accept my wrongs, own my wrongs, and choose to be a better man moving forward in my life. Every experience can serve you. The successful black man is not perfect; he's just compiled his experiences, evolved, and decided what kind of man he is going to be. At a certain point this man knows how he's going to conduct himself in a relationship. He's looking for the same attributes in you. He's made a declaration that he will be present and faithful in his relationships. He's looking to see if your characteristics enable him to trust you in that same regard. You may have not moved that way in your past relationships, but to be compatible with this man you have to able to be calibrated and faithful to him.

Universal Choice

If you are breathing, you can change. If you continue to get unfavorable results in relationships, face yourself and where you continue to fall short. If the need for you to change didn't exist, your relationship outcomes would be more favorable. You would be a better person and choose better people. If we choose to believe lies, we consequently live in the bondage of never escaping the realities and outcomes associated with living the lie. If we choose to live the truth concerning who we are, we are poised for change, and experience the freedom of being an evolved and different version of ourselves, with different and elevated outcomes that are favorable and healthy. This is all facilitated by simply not lying to ourselves, and accepting the reality of the person that stares back at us in the mirror, and taking the necessary measures to ensure a version of ourselves that we are satisfied with will stare back at us when we choose to change.

Do It For You

The best and most lasting change is when you change for yourself and not for other people. When you change for people, often times you don't have a belief in the change that resonates deeply enough with you for it to be lasting. This change is for someone else, and not a result of you being true to yourself. When you change for yourself, even if someone has pointed things out to you that you need to change, you now see the reasoning behind the change and make a personal connection with change improving you as a person, and translating to a better version of yourself moving through life. When this type of change occurs within you, it is real, and the elevated results that surface in your life will be evidence of the authenticity of your change.

Instead of changing for others, change for yourself. You will be the best benefit to others, given you are showing up as not what they want you to be, rather a concretely better version of yourself whose change is lasting and not fleeting to please others. You have to develop a personal relationship with, and see value in changing, in order for it to be lasting. When change makes sense to you, it is time to take steps toward the change you desire to experience.

I can remember times where I was in a new situation with a woman who I desired to be my final dating destination. I expressed to her the changes I needed to see to put me in a place where we could begin a relationship. The changes would be very quick and unsubstantial, as she resorted back to her original behaviors. This occurred because she changed for me, and not for herself. The only way to change for yourself is for whatever is being asked of you has to make sense to you in terms of the overall enhancement of your quality of life. Change has to resonate with you internally, even though an external person brought the need for it to your awareness. Until you develop a personal relationship with the philosophy and ideology behind the change, and it makes sense to you on a personal and spiritual level, outside of people and anything in the material world, change will be fleeting and temporary.

I came to a place of acceptance that the change I desired in the young lady I was dealing with made no sense to her on a spiritual level. It just wasn't her, and she essentially saw nothing wrong with the version of herself that she was taking through life. This is how a man can be patient, but still put credence in the reality of what he sees, and move according to this reality, and not the hope of what could be and emotion.

Pastor Quantrell Smith, of Word Movers Ministry, said something in a message years ago that resonates with me until this day. He said, "You take you wherever you go." To solidify this statement, he gave an example of if a person is a drug addict in Washington, D.C., they can move to Oklahoma and they will find the drug culture there as well. The reasoning behind this statement is that it doesn't matter what environment you are in; it matters what's in you that will manifest itself in any environment. You know you've become the best version of yourself when you influence the environment in the manner you'd like to, and the environment doesn't influence you. This is when you've mastered yourself and subsequently mastered your life.

By and large, whatever a person shows up as is who they will perpetually be moving forward. Very few individuals change, even though every human being has the ability and the capacity to do so. It's commendable when a person can exhibit lasting change. Below are strategies to join the remnant of individuals who harness and embrace their power to change.

Three Strategies For Lasting Change

1. **Face Yourself**

    When you repeatedly encounter circumstances in relationships and in life that just don't go the way you envisioned them going, face yourself. Accept your position in the equation that didn't go your way. Do not stare away from what you see.

2. **Take Ownership**

    Once you have identified your contribution to your perpetual unfavorable circumstances, now you must take ownership of what you saw. Even if you don't think you were capable of whatever was looking back at you when you faced yourself, you exhibited these behaviors. These behaviors are you in this moment. They do not have to be you moving forward. If you did it, it was in you. That level of acceptance sets the stage to be set free from the impediments to experiencing the outcomes you want in relationships and in life.

3. **Make a Declaration**

Once you have faced yourself and accepted the areas in your being and character, that need to change, it is now time to make a declaration as to the type of person you are going to be moving forward in your life. The declaration exemplifies you have accepted who you were and now consciously choose an opposite trajectory and different approach to life. The pivotal element in the establishment of the declaration is the acceptance of everything that you saw staring back at you in the mirror when you faced yourself after experiencing repeated unfavorable outcomes. It's easy to meander through life with no sense of concrete purpose. The declaration changes this, with every movement being purposeful and positioning yourself to experience the desired outcomes that have eluded you. The declaration is the genesis of you showing up in life in a way that is healthy, progressive, and beneficial to individuals who you encounter.

Ye Shall Know The Truth

One of my favorite biblical offerings is: "And ye shall now the truth, and the truth shall make you free." We can encounter the truth, but to acknowledge the truth, and accept the truth, is when you are set free. When you "know" the truth you have gone beyond acknowledgement and entered the realm of acceptance of whatever truth is staring at you. When you know it, you accept it. When you accept it, you experience the corresponding freedom of change. When you are free from bondage your environment immediately changes. When you accept the truth that stares at you, concerning who you are, your entire atmosphere will shift. Your experiences will be purer. Your life will be meaningful and impactful, as you take the best possible version of yourself through it.

Notes and Insights

Matthew C. Horne

Notes and Insights

Chapter
13
Love is Not Enough

Any truly successful man is centered. He is not driven by emotion, because he understands that his greatest impact on the world will be based on his ability to be and remain mentally and spiritually clear. His life's mission and fulfilling it is what his life is centered on. He won't compromise his ability to fulfill that mission, no matter how deep of an emotional connection he has with you. He understands that: where there is no vision the people perish. Where there is vision the people flourish. His God-given purpose is the barometer for all of the decisions he makes. He is bringing you peace and expects that in return. He may interact with you and develop real feelings and emotions for you, but he will choose his purpose if his quality of life is in jeopardy.

The Importance of Change

When a man has patiently gone down a road with you, and desires to see certain characteristics in you over time that will make him feel safe having you in his life forever, and he gets to a place where he is not seeing the changes he hoped for, he'll ask himself, "What will my quality of life be like if this woman remains in my space?" Once the successful black man asks himself this question after patiently working with you in areas you could improve in, he's already checked out of the relationship, even if he's not aware of it yet.

The successful black man is rational. Anything that he asks of you, in relation to personal change, is going to elevate you. He sees certain things that could align better in his elevated world, so subsequently, his desire is to see your knowledge, wisdom, intelligence, and perception of the world around you elevate. The world will look similar to you both, even as you two maintain your individuality. The successful black man is not controlling. He prides himself on extending the opportunity for people to be themselves. He just wants a version of you that is compatible with him and his quality of life.

It's important that whatever is suggested to you from him makes sense to you, and that you are not changing just to please him. Time and vulnerability will reveal the substance behind your change, so it's advantageous to change for the right reasons. The right reason being that aside from appealing to the man in front of you, you can see how your life will be heightened and elevated by moving in accordance with the sound knowledge and wisdom he is offering you. Only make strides toward whatever change is being presented to you if it makes sense to you, and resonates with you on an intellectual and spiritual level. If whatever the successful black man presents to you about ways to improve yourself makes sense to you, it is likely that you two are compatible, paving the way for a lasting union.

Ultimately, you have to be true to yourself. Whatever the man is presenting to you can be as sound of wisdom as you have ever encountered, but you may cherish characteristics about yourself that are not ideal for this man in a relationship. That's why it is important for you to not just immediately implement change into your life; it's beneficial to have a conversation with yourself and see if that particular suggested change makes sense to you. Ask yourself, "Do you value what the successful black man has presented to you, as well as the increase in quality of life you will experience through the implementation of change?" If your answer is, "yes," then move forward. If it is not, then it is best to remove yourself from the situation, because time and vulnerability will reveal your displeasure with whatever is being asked of you, and your enjoyment of remaining exactly the way that you are. This is an issue of pure compatibility and long-term fulfillment together.

He is Not a Dictator

The successful black man is not above reproach. He will filter any suggestions that you believe could benefit the relationship through the same progressions in terms of the overall benefits to his quality of life if he implements what you are saying, and it makes sense to his rational mind. He will give consideration to your wisdom as well, if you have proven yourself to possess a sound mind and are progressive in nature. The successful black man is open to whatever life shows him about himself and is in a perpetual state of growth. His personal greatness is anchored in understanding that having a firm grasp on life, and arriving at a satisfying place in life, doesn't negate the need and desire for endless self improvement. His humility will keep him open to improving. His wisdom and results make him of benefit to those who encounter his guidance.

Life's Twists and Turns

Even when the successful black man is considering you for a long term union, and has a desire for you that grows with an intensity all of its own, he still will take a very prolonged look at you in all of your multi-faceted nature, to ultimately decide if you will compliment him in ways that align with the ideal experience he'd like to engage in over time. The meticulous observation of his potential partner is grounded in the uncertain nature of life. The only stability in life, in relation to things that you do not control, is instability.

The successful black man has experienced many reversals in his life, just as any person has. He is intelligent enough to create as much stability in and around his life to buffer the inevitable challenges life will bring his way. He wants his atmosphere as neutral as possible.

He is too cerebral to voluntarily shake his world up when life is going to deal him many circumstances that have the power to do so. He understands that death can occur to someone close to either one of you, a job could be lost unexpectedly, a challenging health ailment could present itself to either one of you, or your children could go in a direction they weren't raised to go in. Life is life. Life is undefeated in its ability to present challenging circumstances to anyone who breathes air. With this understanding, he is taking an in-depth look at whoever stands in front him, independent of his love for this person.

The Gravity of Marriage

I have young friends who are going through challenging divorces due to them overlooking the red flags they saw in their significant others. Choosing to see the good and ignoring the glaring red flags of instability and questionable behavior is what did the marriage in. What I respect about these friends of mine is their ability to take personal responsibility for their actions. This lets me know these friends are poised for growth, and will not make emotional decisions, and disregard the gravity of the reality of what they see in women moving forward in their lives. They have taken away from their situations and have postured themselves to have an elevated experience with the next woman who potentially could be "The One."

The man I speak of in this book is not perfect in his perception of others, but will assuredly snap out of any love spell and see what is standing in front of him, while moving according with the reality of what he is shown.

Some of my married friends have told me that I can be as perceptive as I can possibly be in evaluating a woman who could potentially be my wife, but there are variables in marriage that you can't prepare for. According to my friends, you can't forecast such things as the loss of someone close to your wife, and the impact it will have on her behavior and mental state moving forward. They include other forms of loss and other devastating life experiences and their effects on a wife in these conversations.

In these conversations with my married male friends, I tell them I agree and disagree. I agree in the regard that you never completely understand a person as long as you are with them, but a person's character over time can make you trust them in any situation they will find themselves in. I explain that whoever my wife ends up being, I will trust her based on the version of herself that she has shown me over time. I trust that over any circumstance that could come her or our way. They still insist that I can't fully predict. I contend that I can find confidence in making the most intelligent and observation-based decision about my spouse, and it will anchor the union in a healthy way, even though no one has the ability to perfectly predict life's unstable and volatile surprises.

Many challenges that some of my friends face in marriage I believe could have been addressed before ever proposing. Issues such as persuading your wife over following the vision you have established for your life and the relationship, are unfathomable to me. Drastically different opinions that concern major areas of life that contribute to overall emotional wellbeing and quality of life are something that I could never see present if I'm going to spend the rest of my life with someone.

Marrying someone solely for love and trusting that many evident wrinkles in the rela-

tionship will iron themselves out is the ultimate wild card.

This is not the sentiment toward marriage of the successful black man. He respects marriage as the most important quality of life decision he will ever make outside of gravitation toward a higher power greater than himself. He will not marry on hope; he will marry knowing that he gave himself a chance at the best quality of life possible based on his prolonged observation of the woman in front of him.

What I respect about my friends who are attempting to get on the same page with their wives, is that they are trying and not surrendering their marriages to conflicts in the area of personal philosophies and compatibility. They may not have had the emotional maturity to understand themselves enough to understand what they were actually compatible with in terms of a spouse when they got married, but as they have grown and matured as men they choose their wives and their families daily in the fight to create the best life and atmosphere possible. These are successful black men, and I salute them.

Most things outside of levels of disrespect from a woman that are irreconcilable, the successful black man will hang in there with you and try to get on a healthy page with you when he is emotionally invested in you. Even if he made an emotional decision to marry you, he won't be rash in his decisions concerning removing himself from it. He respects his commitment to you and to God. His actions are aligned with his commitment. However the pendulum swings in the marriage, he will be satisfied with the valiant effort he undertook to preserve and enhance his union.

Anticipating Versus Reacting

Although I admire the men who are attempting to get on the same page with their wives in their marriages, my philosophy and way of seeing the world is from a preemptive lens and not a reactionary gaze. I respect the man who is finding his way and learning about himself throughout his marriage and relationships, but there is a successful black man who has found himself and consequently understands what attributes in a woman represent compatibility and the long term likelihood of an enjoyable union.

All of his parts are assembled. My question to you is: will you be a version of yourself that resonated deeply with him on many levels as you two encounter one another and progress together? When you are this woman, the love takes on a life force of its own.

Love intensifies when it is harbored in a safe space.

The Quintessential Man

The conversations I have had with my successful young black male friends about dating and relationships made contributions to my offerings in this book. The consensus was that we've all encountered women we really wanted to be with, but the commonalities amongst what we saw all made us say the same thing: "My quality of life is too good to deal with what would assuredly be a relationship that would translate to perpetual turmoil and discourse."

These friends are very educated, intelligent men who are financially well off and solid as individuals mentally, physically, and emotionally. Men with something to lose, meaning a satisfying and substantial life being achieved on their own, will assuredly not fall prey to bringing unnecessary difficulties into their lives. The common characteristics amongst the women we encountered were entitlement, competitiveness, condescending behavior, poor spending habits and money management, and disrespect encapsulated our collective experiences in dating. Notice, I said dating and not relationships. We valued ourselves enough to take a long enough look to decide this type of interaction was not for us, and quickly departed.

If the black man is centered within himself and satisfied with his quality of life, he'll always choose stability over toxic companionship.

To align with the quintessential black man, you want to exhibit these three characteristics:

1. Understand what the dynamics of a healthy relationship look like, and how you must show up to contribute to a healthy and peaceful union.

2. You must desire the healthy and peaceful relationship.

3. The version of yourself that you are must be a match for the quintessential black man, and must facilitate the reality of creating and experiencing healthy relationship dynamics.

His First Choice

The successful black man's first choice in a woman is one who he knows he can have an effortless journey in getting to know. This journey isn't perfect, but it is very apparent, based on how the woman shows up to the interaction, that she is elevated in her thinking and essence. His first choice is a welcomed commodity into his space due to her being a departure from his normal experience with women.

If the version of you that shows up takes pride in your physical appearance and exhibits beauty, and can be experienced by a man as someone who has offered stability over time, he'll not only love you, he'll be enraptured with you resulting from him seeing you as the quintessential woman who he can have his definition of the all encompassing experience with.

Love is powerful. External factors can cause a man's love to grow for you, quickly. A man is already intrigued when he is extremely attracted to you on a physical level and you exhibit a sound mind, coupled with being a departure from his normal draining experience with women. He will develop intense feelings for you when he sees you exhibit healthy characteristics, and actually match the level of energy he gives to you in the interaction, with the physical attraction being mutual. Love will develop between you two over time. Love is amplified and grows with no recourse when the man can easily identify that no barriers inhibit you two from experiencing healthy relationship dynamics. If the man is intensely drawn to you, but sees that there are fixtures present that could be a hindrance to a healthy experience with you, he will be present but reserved in how much of him self he gives to the interaction. He will consciously and unconsciously bring a halt to the emotional advancement of the interaction because emotions are a great feeling, but a high and healthy quality life is the ultimate feeling that he experiences daily based on how he has framed his life.

> **When you have a beauty that is tailored to his eye and enhance his life and quality of life with your presence, then he will long for you.**

When he sees you show up consistently as this version of yourself, his intelligent and cerebral nature will provoke him to identify you as what you are: a departure from his normal experience, and someone to undertake a journey of exclusivity and anticipation with.

Women who fit these criteria do not last long on the dating market. They're in tune with themselves enough to only interact with men of sound mind and virtues, who exhibit healthy characteristics. With her being only calibrated to this type of man, based on the woman she has become, she is in the atmosphere of high caliber men only, as she makes herself available to these types of men exclusively. One of these men will quickly identify her as the gem that she is. He will have thoughts of exclusivity upon meeting her and arrive at that place over time as he observes her. He will see a constant in front of him that represents everything he desires, with these desires being validated as real over time.

Place a version of yourself that fits high level and healthy criteria, in front of a self-aware, high quality man, and you will not escape his presence. The love that he will develop for you will not be inhibited or rivaled by any question marks that may surround you. You will occupy more of his thoughts daily. He will be completely gone with you.

Notes and Insights

Notes and Insights

Chapter 14

It Is Easy To Get Married

Years ago, I saw a video by a youtuber named Rom Wills titled: "The Average Black Woman's Real Competition." Before watching the video, I thought he was referencing women of other races. In actuality, he was saying that a black woman's real competition is black women who are easy to be around, in shape, feminine, non-combative, and classy. He essentially said that these types of women have favorable dating experiences with men, and don't last long on the dating market. What he said, without saying it, is that a man's average encounter with black women results in an experience that is the opposite of the woman he describes.

If you value your appearance, are easy to be around, carry yourself with class, and are feminine, and have or are currently working on resolving your inner trauma, you will not get overlooked by the successful black man.

In Real Time

There was a group of young women in their early twenties that I met at a rooftop establishment in Washington, D.C. a little after the summer of 2019. There was about five of them, with only one being not married. All but one had crowns on their heads and rings on their ring finger. As it turned out, all but one of these women were married, and they were out celebrating the latest of their crew who was about to undertake the journey of matrimony. All of the married women in this crew were wed in the last year, as this group comprised young, newly married women. With the exception of the non-married young woman, they were all very laid back and easy to talk to. I was happy to see so many married young beautiful black women in one space.

I told them how beautiful they all were and one of them engaged in conversation with me, as the others entertained each other. I let her know that I was writing a book to young black women about appealing to successful black men, so they could experience the outcome she was living. She then informed the rest of the crew, who was in close proximity to us, that I was writing a book to young black women about joining themselves to right type of man. All of the married women were excited and showed interest toward my book and its subject matter. I informed them that I would love to converse with them at another time and get their perspective on the subject matter, given that they were successful in marriage. These married women were open to the idea of conversing further.

The one woman who was unmarried was tall and gorgeous. She was stunning. I was getting great energy from all of the married women, but the stunning, unmarried woman immediately offered me resistance when I proposed conversing with them in regard to subject matter surrounding dating and marriage. When I proposed this conversation, the young unmarried woman in the group said this to me: "If you are the expert, why do you need to talk to us?" I responded with, "I wanted to talk with your married friends." She simply said, "Oh," as she knew her attempt to invalidate me was not successful, and she made a complete fool of herself in the process. I excused myself and told the young ladies it was nice to meet them.

If you notice from the story, every very attractive, polite, feminine, easy going, and receptive woman was married. The reality is that the one boisterous, rude, combative, and challenging woman was single. You can't make this stuff up. This moment was telling on many levels, and simply poetic.

Every one of the young, beautiful married women possibly had the same thought as I excused myself from the conversation: "Their friend ran me off." They likely could have also concluded that: "That's why we are married, and she is not." These thought progressions and processes are very probable in their occurrence. Perhaps we all had an unspoken meeting of the minds. I can concretely say that this was my exact sentiment.

I Have A Strong Personality

Many women take pride in being obnoxious and rude to men. They possess the ideology that "A strong man knows how to deal with me!" Only an unintelligent man who doesn't know what a peaceful existence is like would put up with a woman who fits these criteria. I've seen young women proudly exhibit moments of rude and obnoxious behavior in my presence. In knowing some of them, I knew of the lonely, older women that they emulated. It was perplexing that these young women wouldn't have the presence of mind to see the reality of the older women they emulated who proudly carried the torch of being unnecessarily difficult. These women were alone! They were undesirable to the many men who encountered them and decided to exit stage left.

This behavior is not a badge of honor. Real men are not sticking around for this. This is my promise to you based on my experienced lens. This is how you see the gorgeous thirty plus year old woman who you know has guys waiting in a line to approach her, actually be alone. It's the consistent characteristics that she exhibits to men that turn them into Olympic sprinters opposite of her direction. This behavior is immature and will land you with no man at all, or a man you cannot respect who constantly tolerates your disrespect. It's a lose/lose situation if you a desire a healthy and enjoyable union with a man.

He Will Quickly Depart

A couple of weeks ago I had the pleasure of speaking at a dating event that included resources such as psychologists to offer advice on creating healthy relationships. One of the gentlemen speakers was someone I resonated with deeply in relation to his personal philosophy. This gentleman was a licensed mental health professional, possessing more degrees than a thermometer. He said he's arrived at a place in his life, where if women exhibit certain obnoxious behaviors when he meets them, he just departs. He's seen enough and understands what his ideal experience looks like with a woman enough to quickly identify anything that is the contrary to that. He essentially gets turned off immediately when an interaction with a woman begins with him not receiving the same courtesies he is extending to a woman.

> **There are very good, respectful, decorated, and attractive men who may be enamored with your looks, but they will depart from your presence with fleeting foot if your energy toward him is distasteful.**

The Consummate Woman

When a levelheaded, focused, successful, and driven black man meets a woman who fits Rom Will's description of an ideal black woman, he pinches himself because of the departure from his normal experience with the black women he meets. If a black man, who is not bringing a myriad of mess and baggage to the table, meets this type of beautiful, easy going, classy, intelligent, considerate, health conscious black woman, and sees these characteristics, he looks at you from a long-term vantage point, and is eager to gauge the compatibility you two share over time. These are the women who that man, in a relatively short amount of time, recognize as a gem, and a welcomed variance from encounters he is not suited to. In essence, and in appearance, you will check all of his boxes.

He Can Only Be Offered One Thing

The successful black man already has it all. He is self-sufficient and complete. No woman can complete him because he is already whole. Being the consummate woman, his mind is going to be blown by how you showed up and captivated him. It is natural to desire companionship, all the while being happy and content on your own. The whole person presents nothing but themselves to the other person. They don't have to adopt a façade or pretense to impress others because they are enough. When a successful, sound minded, mentally and spiritually whole man sees a woman who is taking no angles with him, and presenting her whole amazing self to him, he'll be enraptured with her, expeditiously.

The safer a man feels with you, meaning that he can focus exclusively on the emotion and connection that you two are establishing, without having to monitor baggage and red flags, the faster his emotions toward you will flourish. If you show up to the life of the successful black man, not perfect, but with all of your parts intentionally assembled and balanced, he'll fall for you without hesitation. He will respect your rarity, and how you turned his already magnificent world upside down, with thoughts of forever with you in close proximity.

Notes and Insights

Notes and Insights

Chapter
15
It Means Nothing To Him

Looks and beauty are obsolete and cannot be used to control and manipulate real men. The successful black man has likely seen and done it all with beautiful women given the place he has elevated himself to. He desires a sustentative experience with a woman that enhances his entire being, independent of appealing to his natural senses.

Many women are used to interacting with weak men, who will tolerate any type of behavior and disrespect from a woman in the name of potential intimate gratification. Not the solid man. He would rather go without the woman who physically appeals to him, than to deal with her in a space of disrespect. Most men do not freely operate in their masculine essence and value themselves enough to require the same treatment from women that they extend to them. The healthy and lasting relationship with a successful black man comes at the expense of bringing the best version of yourself to the interaction, and understanding that any physical prowess you possess will appeal to him, but not dissuade him from straying away from his solid core which is built on self-respect and self-awareness.

Adherence to the repetitive themes in this book regarding the successful black man's irrevocable level of self-respect and self-awareness will be the difference between landing the self-respecting man that represents balance and long term stability, or partnering with the man whose instability is rooted in his lack of self-awareness and self-respect. If you present aspects of yourself that are sustentative to the successful and grounded black man, your house will be constructed on a solid foundation, facilitating the growth of a solid structure.

Your level of beauty and shapeliness does not afford you the leverage to undeservingly mistreat the successful black man who enters your space respectfully. There's an abundance of gorgeous women who have played themselves by mistreating men they were actually into, thinking that all men will bow at their feet, given this is their daily experience with low-value men who they have no interest in.

Another One???

About a year ago, I was at an establishment in Washington, D.C. just unwinding after a day's work. Before long, a tall, gorgeous woman crossed my path and I approached her with no hesitation. She and her collection of female friends were heading toward the exit not too far from where I was standing. I stopped her and she looked up at me and liked what she saw, evidenced in the reality that she had her girls wait on her while the young lady and I conversed. It turned out that this woman was celebrating her 30th birthday that evening, and her friends were showing her a great time. I didn't want to keep her from her waiting party of friends, so we exchanged numbers went on with our respective evenings.

This particular young lady was extremely beautiful and had a height that went well with mine. I am six feet and five inches in height, and she stood a slim but womanly five feet and eight inches in height. My recurring sentiment to tall women when I meet them is that: you can wear whatever heels you'd like with no worries in my presence. I'm direct in my writing, but understand I have jokes, and the comedy is never too far away if I'm around. There was anticipation in the air surrounding this very attractive woman I encountered momentarily.

We sent a few text messages back and forth over the next week or so. She asked to have a phone conversation, so we made it happen the evening that she presented the option. We began to learn about one another during the extended conversation. I never disclose what I do for a living when I meet a woman in person initially. I prefer for the favorable attributes that surround me to exist in the background. I want any woman I meet to be attracted to me and whatever energy and essence that surrounds me in that moment. I believe success should be worn as an undershirt and not on a man's sleeve. It is vital for a man to attract women for the right reasons. None of my material accomplishments and possessions enter the initial conversation unless I am asked. This is the course of action I took in the initial conversation I had with this young lady.

No self-assured man leads in with how wonderful he is and sells his value to a woman based on his material acquisitions and his ranking in the societal tier of success.

You can read more about this thought process in my book *How To Get Beautiful Women ...and Everything Else You Want From Life.*

During this phone conversation, I told the young lady that I am an author and a motivational speaker, and that I also own a Book Publishing and Public Relations company for authors. She told me what she did for a living as well. We both lived in decent proximity to one another, and there seemed to be a mutual anticipation to meet again in person. I was headed out to a friend's birthday gathering, so I informed the young lady I would call her back once I got in my car. She informed me that it was getting late and that she would possibly be asleep by the time I called her. I told her I'd keep my word and call, and that if she didn't answer we could converse another time.

I called when I got in the car and she did not pick up the phone. I left it at that, given she'd likely seen my missed call. A better part of a week went by and I did not hear back from her. She contacted me exactly a week later and texted me, "What happened?" I replied with, "I figured you saw my missed call." She responded with, "Oh, you put the ball in my court?" I responded with, "I only do mutual interest." She then wrote a soliloquy explaining how she saw my missed call and is interested in me, and that she had to focus on preparing to go out of town (insert violin music). By the time in that message exchange where she copped the plea, I was more than turned off. You guessed it; I never replied or said another word to her.

You don't have to look too deeply into that entire scenario to realize that even the men she was into, she still wanted to establish her dominance and value over his. You can easily see that this woman was used to disrespecting men and having them chase after her. When she said, "You put the ball in my court?" you could tell it was an unusual phenomenon for her to meet a self-assured man that valued himself over her radiant beauty. It was telling of how the majority of men really are weak, and regularly compromises their manhood for the privilege of being in the presence of extremely beautiful women. This young lady was astonished that I didn't chase her. She would have never respected me if I called her consecutively after not getting a response from my missed call. The situation was dead at the point of her expecting an over pursuit at the expense of my self respect. A dynamic would have been established that she could disrespect me, and that I would stick around for it. That would have been the beginning of an interaction that would have had a lopsided unhealthy dynamic that favored her.

Pained and Disappointed

I left that interaction pained and disappointed for her as a black woman because I understood the realities that black women face in terms of unfavorable marriage statistics. Figuratively speaking, I could have been her husband. That's where the pain and displeasure existed. Who knows how many solid black men she will encounter in her life that will actually help to mature her and consistently become a better version of herself? I am not God. I do not know what God has in store for that young woman. I do know that it is not an everyday experience to encounter a solid black man that you are actually attracted to and could build toward a healthy and lasting union with.

> **When you have uncommon beauty, it is easy to get lost in the sea of men who approach you daily, but train your eye to recognize the one's you like, and become a version of yourself that is appealing to them.**

He Is Looking For This

Honestly, most men are looking for a woman to be thinking like a woman at the age of twenty-five. I chuckled within myself seeing a thirty-year-old woman operate on this plain of consciousness. When you can process information and move in a mature manner, it is very appealing to the successful black man. I've seen this trait in very young women in their early twenties and have seen it escape women in their forties. In totality, the successful black man does not want to contend with unnecessarily immature and goofy theatrics from women.

Women Will Leave His Presence Better

I have no regrets about how I handled that situation. It's possible that this particular young lady will encounter another solid black man that she is attracted to and move in a more mature manner with him, setting the stage for a more favorable experience than her and I had. If I would have done anything differently with her, I would have failed her. She left the interaction knowing that there exist men who value themselves enough to walk away from any foolishness that she will present to them. I extended an opportunity to look in the mirror and decide how she will conduct herself the next time a man that she finds appealing and attractive enters her space. Her gaining the awareness that high-value men do exist, and how to conduct herself with them translates to her being a better version of herself. This brings me great satisfaction that she is possibly poised to move differently the next time a similar scenario finds her.

Dynamics Revisited

I recently had a conversation with a very young black woman in her early twenties. We were in a relaxed setting and conversing. We began discussing how the initial impression a man makes on her determines how she views and proceeds with the man. This young woman fully understood and articulated that if she sensed weakness in a man, stemming from her ability to walk all over him, she will categorize him as the man she can disrespect, and proceed to take advantage of him accordingly.

Any person, young or old, understands that relationships dynamics are established in the beginning of an interaction. It is common knowledge that isn't always applied due to the fear of losing whoever is in front of you.

This young woman also explained to me during our conversation that she cannot respect a man that she can disrespect, nor can she look to him for strength long term if he doesn't operate from a place of strength. This young woman laid out what many know, but rarely acknowledge concerning relationship dynamics.

This is why the successful black man will make his exit when he receives unwarranted disrespect from a woman he is interacting with. This is true concerning both younger and older black men.

The successful black man quantifies behaviors he has encountered and associates them with favorable and unfavorable outcomes.

He is not meandering through life; this is how he sizes up women and situations quickly to only place himself in desirable positions.

Believe me, he's dealt with disrespectful women, listened to them cop pleas, only to see them disrespect him again soon after. He knows how the story ends, so he removes himself from the story when he sees is taking shape.

The First Time

If you truly desire a successful, self-aware, and grounded black man, get it right with him the first time. Once certain lines of disrespect have been crossed, especially in the beginning when dynamics are being established, there's no coming back from it. It's actually all uncomplicated; if a man that you are into enters your space, in a respectful way, give him the same energy.

Men Like This

Any man who thinks he can treat you any kind of way because he is successful, and has favorable attributes, is not the successful black man that I describe in this book. You don't have to settle just because a man has a lot going for him and doesn't feel he has to be accountable in any way.

Unhealthy relationship dynamics do not just randomly materialize one day in the relationship. There are signs early on. Precursors and behaviors were present in the beginning. If we experience unhealthy relationship dynamics, we signed up for them. This is why you have to become more aware from interaction to interaction with men. You will be more aware of their consequences if ignored. The knowledge of how you contribute to them will become apparent. The symptoms that lead to these dynamics will be glaring if presented to you. Your exit ramp will effortlessly appear when you encounter these attributes. If your goal is personal growth, you will despise the toxic characteristics within yourself that contribute to unhealthy relationship dynamics, and consciously and intentionally rid yourself of them.

A progressive initial practice when encountering the man that you are into is to give respect when you are given respect. Once respect is given and interest and attraction are present, the man will gladly walk with you, placing one foot in front of the next. Anticipation will be his stance toward you. A sunset may await you two.

This Means Everything To Him

The successful black man is a purpose driven individual. He has never "arrived" in his mind, regardless of how much success and worldly possessions he has accumulated. Nothing supersedes his ability to carry out his purpose. Him being able to do that, while you two share a space, is eminent in his thoughts and carries a reality of importance. He has a God consciousness and needs to be able to carry out the instructions from His Manufacturer.

A large component of compatibility, in his mind, is the ability to maintain the necessary atmosphere, entrenched in peace, to be able to carry out his purpose on a continual basis. This means more to him than any amount of beauty he could ever be presented with. He's too conscious of himself, and too cognizant of his purpose, to voluntarily introduce something into his world that would compromise that.

This is how he cannot be controlled or manipulated by anything a woman presents or offers to him. He has a higher desire than having a woman in his life, while possessing the innate desire to be with a woman who suits him. Many men make exceptions for beautiful women; he won't.

Your beauty and other amazing attributes are enjoyable and enticing to him. In reality, the beauty is what motivates any man to begin an interaction with you. The highest importance is that you are bringing an emotionally healthy, available, evolved, and self-assured version of yourself to him. Everything else about you is temporal and irrelevant.

Notes and Insights

Notes and Insights

Chapter 16

Decided Advantages

Hate and love cannot coexist. Hate will always be the stronger of the two variables. Some of the most physically beautiful women I have encountered have been the most emotionally and mentally damaged. After seeing this repeatedly I had to ask myself: "Why is this so?" After seeing certain patterns in various situations involving young beautiful women, I began to stare at what I saw, and draw conclusions as to why this is.

In one particular situation I found myself in with an extremely beautiful young woman, it all made sense. She possessed intelligence, beauty, and a radiant presence. Many people around her, from family to acquaintances, said unbelievable things to her to lower her self-esteem, and dissuade her from believing she could have the various blessings that the hand that God dealt her afforded to her. It made sense to me given my experiences being extremely young, fresh out college, authoring books endorsed by some of the top speakers in the world. Peers, as well as elders who I admired and respected, pulled out all of the stops to get me to abandon my calling, and consequently, forfeit all the blessings I experienced immediately when I bypassed every fallacy about me they attempted to sell me. Consequently, I entered into my rightful space that my gifts, talents, and attributes afforded me.

When I saw this young lady go through unthinkable attempts to sabotage her future, the reasoning behind it came into full clarity: she had the world going for her, and eventually, if she stayed her course, the world would be hers. The phrase "decided advantages" is what I deduced from seeing her experience while being in very close proximity to her. Everyone around her was scared beyond measure that she would outperform them in life. When I absorbed the gravity of what she had to offer to the world, and the likelihood of her arriving at her designed and ordained space, it was awe-striking. She was special, and everyone knew it.

Young, beautiful women, you may have wondered why your treatment in life has been preferential in ways, as doors have opened effortlessly for you that were not ajar for others, while experiencing unexplained vitriol and hate from those closest to you, as well as perfect strangers. Who you are, coupled with how you are packaged, and the glaring potential that people around you understand better than you do, is the culprit.

Decided advantages are powerful and dangerous. When you have extremely rare qualities, they intimidate people both young and old. I'm writing this to bring clarity and sense to something that has been so consistent in your life, with the logic behind it escaping you. Your presence brings the best and worst out of people. You never know which side the pendulum will swing from person to person, so you may dim your light as best as possible to go unnoticed. If you are going to take full advantage of your decided advantages, your stance must be unapologetic when utilizing that advantages that God gave you.

How To Take Advantage

You take advantage of your decided advantages by having a perception of yourself that aligns with the makeup that God gave you. If your opinion of yourself does not align with the reality of how God constructed you, you will never experience the full benefit of what people around you see very clearly is at your disposal.

The more physically beautiful that you are, the stronger you have to be, given that beauty has been a facilitator for exceptional experiences since the beginning of time.

Extreme beauty is a door opener. Socially acceptable and celebrated appearances have been attacked since people and insecurities ever existed. Your only hope to maximize any decided advantages you've been given is to always maintain a healthy perception and opinion of yourself. People's words, vitriol, and hate cannot influence you when you are at one with yourself, your purpose, and potential.

Going through life now and experiencing long standing success, I have experiences every so often that place me back into the scenes of the beginning of my journey to success. When I was dealing with this particular young lady, and saw her experiences, it was as if I was catapulted back to when I experienced the same attempts on my potential as she was facing.

When I was twenty-two years old, I received my first book contract to co-author a book in my last semester of college. I graduated, and before the co-authored book was released, I began writing my first solo book, *The Universe Is Inviting You In*. Everyone around me knew I was going to be a motivational speaker. The book contract came out of nowhere, but I accepted it. My confidence and knowledge in actually writing a remarkable chapter in this book, and interacting with the publisher, fueled me to undertake the writing and publishing of my first solo book. I was twenty-two years old and I wasn't just writing aimlessly; I also had the talent and anointing to construct a message that was impactful and far beyond my years.

With this being my reality, when people near and far heard I was writing this book, it scared them senseless.

> **You often don't get people's worst toward you until your glimpses of potential begin to teeter into the realm of eminent reality.**

Someone very close to me, who I figured would support me said, "My stomach cringes every time you talk about that book." Individuals in high positions with global reach attempted to discourage me from completing my book saying, "No one is going to buy your book." This was accompanied by other prominent people spewing the words, "What makes you think you can do this." As pathetic as this was on their part, it was more so perplexing given the age difference between us was more than the actual years I existed on the earth. Some of these people were thirty years older than me, and were very accomplished and decorated. I couldn't make full sense of it, but I knew instinctively that whatever they saw in me was real if it had the power to elicit this level of sabotage toward me.

I escaped these attempts on my advantages and potential by never agreeing with what these people said about me. My opinion of myself was greater than the hate filled opinion that was being presented to me. I maintained a healthy perception of myself, listened to timely and uplifting messages daily, and went on to release *The Universe Is Inviting You In* to a global reception, with an endorsement on the front cover from the top African-American Motivational Speaker at the time, Les Brown.

That was amazing, but my level of talent and gifting, coupled with my belief in who God made me, is what facilitated me to be an author of two globally selling books before I was twenty-four years old.

> **If the story in your mind doesn't match the reality of your potential, your potential will remain potential, with the jealousy fueled messages pertaining to you being your eminent beliefs.**

These people who attack your intelligent, beautiful self are attempting to infiltrate your mind with a story that will rob you of every blessing that God intended for you when He created you exactly the way He did. There's divine intention behind your beauty, intelligence, and radiance. Believe the right story concerning who you are, and every ounce of potential that threatens people around you will be fulfilled.

The Power and Magnitude

You won't combat the attempts on your potential until you understand the power and the magnitude of the attempts on the complexion of your life moving forward. The reality is that people's words and attempts on your potential can angle your life into an unfavorable trajectory if you fall prey to it. You are responsible for the story in your mind. Claim your life and your mind so that you will become everything that detractors know you are deep down.

The magnitude that surrounds the attempts on your opinion of yourself, are life-altering. When someone concludes that you have a decided advantage over them, based on some sort of attribute that you possess, they ultimately implore vicious tactics to keep you in a place where you'll never surpass them. You're going through life, focusing on your goals, and regularly are met with unwarranted nasty behavior from people. They see something in you that represents a life, or experience, they could never have. Instead of them thanking God for the advantages and attributes He bestowed upon them, they'd rather keep you from experiencing the things that are exclusive to your path and calling. You will see this behavior coming from the most unsuspecting people. Don't worry about where it is coming from; instead, focus on the reality of the action that is presented to you, and the power it has to damage you if you falter to hate filled rhetoric and actions toward you. Develop and maintain a healthy perception of yourself.

> **The story in your mind dictates the story of your life.**

Perspective

There is something very positive in this harsh reality I've conveyed in this chapter. What do these people see in you that make them act in such a distasteful manner toward you? Why are attempts being made at your self-esteem when you are minding your business and provoking nothing in this manner? Embrace what they see in you. If you aren't harming others in a way that deserves this level of negative energy coming toward you, then stare at the reality of why you are constantly being presented with illogical attempts on your mind concerning who you are. There's something amazing and uncommon in you. If you can make it past the toxic reality of the attempts at your self-perception, you will see what they see: an amazing individual who God has dealt an unparalleled hand to. Once you change your perspective in these undesirable experiences, you will see what jealous and intimidated individuals don't want you to see: your advantages afford you the best experiences life has to offer. Embrace the reasoning behind the attacks, and not the intention behind them, and you will see the endless open road that is exclusive to just you.

Jealousy Revisited

The worst type of jealousy that exists is when someone looks at you and concludes that they can never have what you have.

This jealousy reveals itself consistently in people in both covert and overt ways. Jealousy cannot be contained, and the root of it, a conclusion that you have advantages they don't believe they can possess, is dangerous. People blossom in different ways as life progresses. Your ascension may not be well received by people in close proximity to you, as well as those off in the distance. Either way, your solace and clarity of mind is preserved when you distance yourself from people who consistently reveal their disdain for whatever your perceived advantage is over them.

When your potential becomes reality, you will see the sentiments of people toward you revealed. Potential makes people feel safe, because we all have it. Very few people maximize the potential of how they were packaged and gifted to fulfill it. Given this, realizing your potential makes many people uncomfortable, and brings about rewards in life many people don't experience. When you come into the fullness of who you are and command every blessing that is congruent with this evolution, you will see both admiration and vitriol. It's par for the course.

You want to exercise enough emotional intelligence to decipher how people feel toward you, and understand the gravity of the decision to not remove yourself from the space of individuals who are intimidated by what you embody, and will go to lengths to ensure you never arrive at the places in life that represent increase. In their mind, your success casts a shadow on them. Jealousy is dangerous. The depths that people are willing to go to inhibit your ascension in life is not quantifiable, and often costly if you didn't have the fortitude and foresight to remove it from your space. Life is easier for some based on the hand that God dealt them than it is for others. You don't deserve to be punished for however God molded your clay. Surround yourself with individuals who revere and anticipate your presence, and the Potter, your Creator, will afford you every experience that aligns with how He constructed you.

Positive Surroundings

Keep positive people and positive energy around you. This environment will foster the maximum potential of everything you were designed to offer to this world. The energy of surroundings is paramount in keeping you in a great and magnetic place for the right people and experiences to enter your space.

You don't always have to be around people who are "on your level" in terms of societal accomplishments and posturing. If a person reveres you and you reverence their presence, that is all that matters.

Being around people who have a positive attitude toward you, and with whom you share a mutual sense of appreciation, creates

> **a healthy environment that fosters the manifestations of your personal greatness.**

When you see this sentiment toward you not being displayed, get out!

If you see the mixture of love and hate displayed toward you, restructure the relationship with distance and completely remove yourself from the situation.

> **It's difficult to give this world your best when people who do not desire that for you remain in your space.**

In my experience, I've received windfall blessings when the toxicity was removed from my space. I've had to restructure relationships with people I would have never suspected I would have. You will either call black, black, or black, blue. One carries a reward, while the other is pandora's box filled with wildcards.

Surrounding yourself with positive people and internalizing uplifting messages aligns your mind, essence, and spirit to match the capacity of the advantages that are given to you. When all of this aligns, you can take full advantage of the advantages you've been dealt.

Toxicity Seeps

Being around toxic people for extended periods of time, I learned that toxicity seeps into, and negatively affects, any person it comes into contact with. If you desire a peaceful experience in life and solid mental health, you never want to spend prolonged periods of time with toxic individuals, if that is within your control. If you keep company with the toxic individuals who have the sentiment of hate and jealousy toward you, you will, in turn, become toxic.

You want to always develop and maintain a healthy perception of yourself. You also want to create internal and external conditions that facilitate you showing up to people, situations, and circumstances in a healthy way. You cannot control what is presented to you, only what you internalize. The acceptance of this mantra will allow you to show up in life stable with a value of yourself that aligns with self-aware and self-respecting people. You will be congruent with the right types of individuals, and have an enjoyable life experience, resulting from you consciously controlling your internal and external atmosphere.

How Does He See You?

The successful black man understands that you can not select family and certain unfavorable life experiences that were bestowed upon you. The successful black man is impressed and put at ease when he sees toxicity around that could have negatively affected you, but it didn't. When he sees your space is welcoming and healthy, he understands that he doesn't have to contend with unnecessary hardships by being with you. What you experienced in life versus what you've become is a barometer in his mind concerning how safe of a space you occupy.

The successful black man is rare and is a blessing to the woman he joins himself to. There will be individuals who make attempts to thwart your mind away from the reality of the well-put-together man who stands before you. He is not concerned with those attempts. He only focuses on the amount of power those attempts have over you.

When he sees that every attempt to skew your view of him was ineffective, he'll respect you as someone who regulates your space. A compromised space leads to instability and chaos. His space is embodied by stability and peace.

If you can regulate your space in a way that toxicity has no entryway, he will acknowledge and admire your strength as a person. Moving this way is indicative of emotional maturity, self-assuredness, and many other desirable traits that translate to a favorable experience with you.

If you can effectively regulate your space, he will feel safe sharing one with you.

What He Wants For You

The successful black man wants nothing but the best for the woman he fancies. Any attributes that are viewed as threatening to the world around you, he will embrace and celebrate them openly and consistently. He wants you to arrive at full bloom. He will speak to your potential and admire the enormity of who you are and the totality that surrounds your potential.

A real man is not threatened by a woman with advantageous attributes.

His stance is celebratory. He will speak life into you, and endlessly expose the world around you, so you can navigate it in a healthy manner.

Pay attention to the man who enters your world with this stance toward you. If he proves himself over time, consider what he says and what he sees. The successful black man is calculated and cerebral. He did not just arrive at a place of success. He is in your future. He can see the effects of internalizing the right and wrong things that are presented to you. He wants you at your best. He needs you as the best version of yourself to ensure an elevated and enjoyable experience for you two. He wants you centered, not perfect. He will see enough in you, if you are the object of his affection, to help propel you to a place where you are internally and externally aligned with everything that God has for you. His knowledge will elevate your quality of life over time, as he is submitted to His Creator who instills wisdom in him. He'll give his best to you to ensure every advantage you've been dealt manifests into a tangible reality.

Notes and Insights

Notes and Insights

Chapter 17
Calibrate Yourself

The beginning of calibrating yourself to the successful black man is becoming the woman who actually desires the traits that the successful black man possesses. Calibration only serves you if it is to the type of man you can have a lasting and healthy relationship with. Desiring any other type of man will be to your detriment and leave you more damaged than you were before you encountered that man.

Calibration is identifying every trait and characteristic that you desire in a man, and then becoming the match for each of those characteristics.

If you are not a match for what you desire, you exist in a fictional reality.

Anticipate

The thing about life is that when you are in a position to react to something, it is often times too late. The best stance to take in life is one of anticipation. This anticipatory stance ensures that you are postured to take full advantage of blessings that enter your life with the capacity to elevate your quality of life and catapult you to realms you never knew existed.

The caliber of black man I describe in this book leaves some women asking: "Exactly where is this man?" I'm almost done writing this book, so I've found myself, in regular conversation with black women, concerning many topics from these pages. Some women think this man is a fallacy, but I explain to these beautiful, black women that he exists. It's abundantly clear that the amount of successful black men pales in comparison to successful black women. My stance to you, as well as the women I've discussed this book with as I've been writing it is: If you desire a man who possesses the characteristics of the successful black man, why not prepare for him if he is so rare? You are going to cross paths with solid black men who you can have the healthy and lasting relationship with. Why not identify the traits that you desire in a man, and align yourself internally and externally to this man? From my vantage, it is pure deductive reasoning. When I explain it from this standpoint, it begins to make sense to women, and my desire is that my assertion resonates with you as well.

Endlessly Improve

Calibrating yourself to the successful black man requires work. The evidence that work is required on your behalf is that you have likely crossed paths with a man who fits the criteria I presented in this book, and that calling him yours has eluded you. At a point and time, it has to resonate that if the desires within you have not become tangible realities, some personal work needs to be undertaken.

Seventy-two percent of black women being projected to be married, ever, as of 2019 is a startling statistic if you desire marriage at all, let alone to a successful black man. It makes sense to become the most appealing version of yourself so his decision to explore a life with you is effortless.

If you think you can just show up any way into the life of the successful black man, and he will be so awe struck with your beauty and

> **desirable qualities that he will welcome you into his world, you are mistaken.**

His mindset is healthy and futuristic. He will not voluntarily dismantle his world in the name of a woman wrapped in desirable external packaging. He is too cerebral, experienced, observant, and intelligent for that.

He desires you. Gravitating to, and desiring, exists on two completely different planes. On which side of this spectrum the successful black man sees you is dependent on how you show up in his life. Possessing the mindset that you can show up in the successful black man's life in any emotional, spiritual, and mental condition will have him view you as emotionally immature, delusional, and entitled. If you are whole in each of those areas, or diligently working toward a place of oneness, he will acknowledge the humility and maturity it takes to undertake a journey toward the best version of yourself. Your presence will be glaring.

His Threshold

Every human being is constructed differently. You don't know the level of patience that resides in the successful black men you encounter.

> **If a man sees enough in you, in terms of attraction and potential, he will stick around and attempt to elevate your thinking, self-awareness, and overall perception of the world.**

If you have identified the areas that have kept you out of healthy relationships, then the successful black man will deduce quickly that he doesn't have to keep you at a distance, while he figures out how much work you will require.

When you are not postured to the successful black man when you two cross paths, it's likely that the man will excuse himself from the situation, given what he has seen over the years in his experiences with women. His willingness to work through whatever inhibits you from functioning in a healthy relationship will depend on many variables, such as age and his overall desire for you. Every man will perform his own calculations to see if the equation that comprises the two of you makes sense to him. No two men are exactly alike. It is a given that if he sees something egregious in the form of disrespect, or glaring red flags from you upon meeting you, he will unapologetically choose his peace and quality of life.

Not being ready for the successful black man when you encounter him is a wildcard in terms of the man's willingness to remain in your space. When everything is taken into consideration there is no need to place the man you desire in a position where he has an abundance of variables that he has to weigh concerning you. The most advantageous stance for you to undertake is to be calibrated to him. He will easily recognize you as being congruent to him, and how you showed up in his space essentially makes the decision for him to explore something meaningful with you, easy.

The Match

When the successful black man sees promise in you, coupled with questionable characteristics that could prove detrimental down the road, he'll keep you at an emotional distance, even when he is present in your life.

He understands that emotions complicate his ability to make a solid conclusion as to who stands before him. An example of this would be a man dating a woman exclusively, but not making her his significant other until he knows they can coexist in a healthy and peaceful space.

When all of your parts are already assembled upon you two meeting, his mind goes to pairing with you in a relationship capacity, and seeing if you two can grow together, and maintain the level compatibility necessary to do it for a lifetime. You showing up calibrated means that he will fully insert himself in the relationship you two share.

There's a different level of emotional depth released from a man when he knows his quality of life will not be negatively affected by regularly interacting with you.

Examine Yourself

To determine whether you are a match for the man you desire, you must undertake personal reflection. There are boxes the man you desire must check. Transversely, you must ask yourself if you check those boxes. This is where the truth sets you on a path to personal freedom.

If you can honestly say that you are a match for the man that you desire, then you deserve an optimal experience with the quintessential man. If you are not a match for the traits and attributes you celebrate in the man you desire, this is an opportunity to mature emotionally and take the necessary measures to calibrate yourself to the man you desire.

Certain personal traits and characteristics you have no control over. If you are five feet and three inches in height, and you desire a man over six feet, that man is your match given that this is what you desire, and that making yourself taller is out of your control. Society may say you two will look awkward together, but if that is what you desire, then set your level there, as this is what brings you fulfillment.

If you desire a financially aware man who is adept at managing money, and you show up into his life with mountains of debt, and a propensity to mindlessly add to it, you are not in touch with reality. This man will easily conclude that whatever he has built financially will crumble if your attitude toward money doesn't mirror his.

Whether all of your parts are assembled in a way that compliments how you'd like your desired man to be constructed, or they are not, you still have a chance to be the successful black man's match.

These three steps will facilitate your movement in that direction:

1. Examine yourself.

2. Take a prolonged and honest look at what you see.

3. Take the necessary measures to act in accordance with what you determine about yourself.

Surrounded By Successful Black Men

You are responsible for consistently being in the presence of successful black men. This occurs by you being the equivalent for every trait and attribute that you desire from the successful black man, in addition to valuing and understanding yourself enough to not keep prolonged company with men who do not fit these criteria.

This is how you create an environment of successful black men. You simply do not entertain men that aren't compatible with the person you've evolved into who is not a match for you. This is completely within your control, and it will manifest itself as long as what you desire is within intelligent reason.

When the successful black men you interact with see who you are, and how you are packaged they'll easily and naturally gravitate toward you. His sentiment toward you will be one of anticipation, and "where have you been."

It's a luxury for a man to find a woman who is conscious of what she had to reconcile, internally and externally, to be the match for the high value man.

My firsthand account is that there are many women the successful, high value black man has encountered that he wished was his final dating destination, only to take a look at her and decide that joining himself with her was not an intelligent decision. It may be something he concluded after a week, or six months. It is quality of life over everything for the successful black man. Given this is his foreboding thought concerning the women he considers, how advantageous is it for you to take the healthiest version of yourself through life?

If you are in optimal physical and emotional condition, the successful black man will immediately recognize your rarity. His consistent experiences are a departure from the type of woman who compliments him. He is intelligent enough to not let you get away, if the desire and attraction for you is present.

Also understand, the spark must be present as well. You will not be it for every man, as every man will not be it for you, regardless of the packaging. The likelihood of you attaining what you want in the type of man you truly desire is heightened when you understand the advantage you give yourself by already being calibrated to what you desire in a man.

> **Nothing is guaranteed; but we all serve ourselves in having the experiences we'd like to have, when we present a version of ourselves to the world that aligns with our desires.**

Boxes

Every woman's ideal man is the one who checks all of her boxes. When you understand the role that you have in experiencing that man, the likelihood of the experience is probable.

Your highest level of fulfillment is in being with a man that you feel you didn't have to settle for. When a man proposes to you, he has concluded that you are the best option for him in every facet of his life, and that no other woman can offer the experience to him that you can offer, and that the emotional depth he's developed for you is unrivaled. Essentially, you check all of his boxes.

What I've witnessed, in close proximity, is women accepting the proposal, while knowing that this man is completely gone with them emotionally, and the sentiment is not shared. This usually doesn't play out well, as the woman hangs in there as long as she can before her desire for what she really yearns for overtakes her, and she departs in hopes of getting all her boxes checked.

You don't have to be this woman if you calibrate yourself to be the match for the man you desire. You can get it right the first time, with no thoughts of what could have been, as you wake up every day to your ideal man.

Women who are the best physical, spiritual, and emotional versions of themselves rarely tend to get overlooked, and don't last long on the dating market. That's how you can see an extremely gorgeous woman alone as she is getting older. There is something alarming that men conclude when interacting with her that sends them packing. Transversely, you can see an attractive woman who doesn't possess earth-shattering beauty in a union with a high quality and attractive black man.

The successful black man has access to the earth-shattering beauties, but in many cases, he partners with a woman who is attractive, who many would say is ordinary. The reality is that the less attractive woman gave him the overall experience he desired. She was calibrated and made his decision to join himself with her a no brainer.

Where you end up in the dating spectrum with successful black men is largely within your control.

Captivated

Many women have voiced to me that very successful men are preoccupied with things other than settling down. Many men have so many options that they're comfortable in that lifestyle. My response to these women is that no man is beyond being captivated by the right woman. Many men meet women at the most unexpected and inopportune times. I've experienced this as I was in a relationship two months after a relationship that I'd been in for three years concluded. You never know when or how it is going to happen. You just want to happen to the right man, with all other variables being irrelevant, as your presence is undeniable.

It's safe to say that British actor Idris Elba is one of the most desirable black men in the world. Idris Elba was married from 1999 to 2003. In an Essence Magazine interview he made this statement: "Am I ever gonna get remarried? I don't think so. Yeah, I don't think so," he told the magazine last July. "Marriage is an institution of sorts. And I've done it. It's not for everybody. It's not my life's calling." This statement was made in 2017. He then goes to Canada to film a movie, enters a jazz theater, locks eye with a beautiful black woman, and is engaged a year later. His sentiment was one of never marrying again, to being engaged a year later.

It's safe to say that he was gone with this beautiful black woman who entered his life, and that he immediately recognized her.

You captivate a man by being packaged in a way that unintentionally disrupts his world.

If you are calibrated properly to the man you desire, he will undoubtedly be captivated.

Matthew C. Horne

Notes and Insights

Notes and Insights

Chapter 18

Emotional Availability

Emotional availability is based on self-awareness and self-respect. Self-awareness is intertwined with emotional availability because you know yourself enough to only have extended interactions with men who are looking for the same things as you are. You are in tune enough with your desires, that naturally you have a clear definition of how a man should move in your space; so, you are only available to the men who operate in this manner. Self-respect is pivotal to emotional availability because men who aren't bringing your same level of energy, effort, consistency, and respect to the table as you are quickly dismissed from the equation.

Any single woman who is always emotionally available is so because she is governed by the traits of self-awareness and self-respect. Her atmosphere is always clean, internally and externally, because she effectively governs her space, and always has an environment that is appealing and welcoming to the successful black man, who shares the mutual emotional availability.

His Take

The successful black man is governed by these traits as well, and never has a woman lingering in his space that is not available to him the same way that he is available to her. He doesn't freely extend his emotional energy and availability that is reserved for women who epitomize what he is looking for and bring the same level of interest and availability to the interaction. He understands how not being fully present when the right woman crosses his path can prove detrimental, given the rarity of women who check all of his boxes, and share a common emotional connection and physical attraction. Quite frankly, he knows his value and will settle for nothing less, independent of how beautiful the packaging is that any woman arrives in.

The Scenario

Here is a common scenario that I've seen play out. A woman meets a man that she is highly attracted to. They hit it off and feelings between them begin to develop intensely, bypassing either one of their expectations. Things progress at a rapid pace, as they are in constant contact with one another. They share an anticipation of each other's presence. The man, who keeps lopsided dynamics with women away from him, feels the energy is not the same from her end. He understands that things progressed quickly between them, and they both were dating people prior to meeting one another.

The conversation is now different given that real feelings have developed. Initially it was okay to date other people, as you two were not together, and real feelings had not made an entrance into the equation. The woman mentioned in the beginning that she was dating casually and had an interest in one man in particular.

The time comes when the man acknowledges that the dynamic of their relationship has changed given the level of increased emotions involved. She explains that she has more intense feelings for the man that she expressed she had an interest in when they initially met. She says to him that she is undecided about how she feels about him.

She further explains that she had been dating this guy for the better part of a year and he chose to keep her at a distance, while she knew she had shown him enough of herself for him to choose her to be in a relationship. She desired a relationship with this man, but he in turn said he needs to place his focus elsewhere. Yet, he still keeps an eye on her to make sure no other man gets too close to her, while he can remain indecisive and maintain his freedom to move however he'd like to.

The new man in her life, who is emotionally available, with any woman he was dealing with before her, knowing her role in his life was not serious, understands fully why there were times where the energy wasn't reciprocated that he was giving to her. He deduces very quickly that he is moving toward her in an uninhibited manner, and she is incapable of moving toward him in the same fashion, because she has a deep emotional attachment to a man that is playing with her.

He then takes a deeper look and realizes that this new woman he fancies does not have a healthy perception of herself, evidenced in her inability to completely disconnect from the man in her life who is literally playing with her. He expresses that he will not be in contact with her regularly moving forward, as he deserves a woman who is just as available to him as he is to her. She senses that this man respects himself and is not willing to be a third wheel in her immature game. She acknowledges that she can already feel him pulling back, and in a desperate attempt to keep the two men in her life that she has real feelings for, she professes how deep her feelings are for him, when moments prior she stated she was unsure of the balance of the emotions she felt for both men.

He understands that his emotion for her is uninhibited, while her emotion toward him exists in duality. Shortly thereafter he acknowledges that he is departing this equation, because he deserves better than what she can offer him. His self-awareness and self-respect prevailed over the emotion he felt for this woman. He made the healthy decision to choose himself and cut contact with the young lady. He point blank explained to her that if you are considering a man who is moving away from you, versus the man who is present and consistent in your life, then that is the type of man you are calibrated to. He expresses to her that you two are likely in love and should probably work things out. He makes a permanent departure, with all lines of communication being nonexistent, as he healthily chooses himself.

This is an all-too-often scenario. This young lady is now left with the man who is playing games with her, pushing her away, while keeping her at arms length. She lost the successful black man who was present, moving toward her, and expressing thoughts to her of them potentially sharing a future together, for the indecisive boy who pushed her away when she expressed her desire for a relationship with him, while keeping tabs on her to make sure no one else got too close to her. If this relationship solidifies, it will be based on instability, possessing the shakiest of foundations.

She had a shot at the real deal: a healthy and lasting relationship with a solid man. She just wasn't calibrated to it.

The solid man who left her life did so because he knew he would become her if he stayed. He knew that he would be emotionally unavailable if the emotionally available and mentally healthy woman he desired would cross his path. He is the best version of himself, and regularly interacts with the type of women he desires. His decision is not the one he wanted to make, but it wasn't the most difficult either, given he valued himself and knew he'd meet another woman, even more gorgeous, with a higher interest in him.

Both get the result of what they are calibrated to. They each experience outcomes based on how they see themselves. She could have easily had this successful black man given his level of emotion toward her that took on a life of its own. He was captivated, but intelligent enough to understand what she represented long term. She was unstable and insecure. He saw the rollercoaster that awaited him, that would totally disrupt the stable, peaceful, and prosperous life he's created for himself. His instincts that have been developed from him taking away from his life experiences, easily allowed him to see around the corner, and view the unhealthy and unstable life that awaited him if he partnered with her. Her picture, in no way, fit within his frame. He exited stage left, as his canvas is reserved for women who adorn it with open road and sunsets.

Reverse

Had the young lady entered this successful black man's life fully available, based on his level of connection and interest in her, they would have had a fighting chance at a sunset. If there were no inhibitions in her ability to come toward him the same way that he was coming toward her, his only focus would have been observing the type of person she was over time, and allowing the emotions between them to intensify due to him having nothing in the back of his mind he had to contend with concerning her.

When intense attraction exists, coupled with the purity of availability from both parties, real magic is on the horizon.

A Healthy Space

When the energy, attraction, anticipation, reverence, and respect are shared between two individuals in an uninhibited manner, two emotionally available and intelligent people will not push the other away. They will acknowledge the rarity and emotional intelligence in one another, and easily conclude that they are each other's final dating destination. Your ability to appeal to, and partner with, the quintessential man is all based on how you show up in his life.

There are women who I have encountered who could have easily been my wife. I had to choose myself based on how these women showed up in my space. I was able to determine that they would not compromise my ideal world, because I had gotten to know and respected myself enough to understand what my ideal space was comprised of.

You are in control of your space. When you absorb this realization, you will never blame anyone who infiltrates in an unhealthy and non-progressive manner. When you develop this thinking, you will in turn develop yourself enough to understand what belongs in your space, and what should be effortlessly dismissed. When you have an understanding of, reverence, and respect for yourself, your space will reflect that. Your space will always be clean and facilitate the right type of people to show up in it. You can't cherish and understand the gravity of your space until you create it. You can't create it until you develop yourself enough to understand the importance of it.

Your space and life are in perfect balance when you take responsibility for the outcomes in your life. Every decision is now meaningful and calculated because you understand what your ideal experience is, and consequently, will not settle for anything less than that. Only then is your healthy space established and maintained, due to you maintaining a healthy perception of yourself. Work on yourself endlessly. You will then create your world, your way.

Emotional Maturity

Letting guys play with you is the easiest way to remain emotionally unavailable. The all encompassing match for the successful black man is the emotionally available woman who is available due to her ability to quickly identify and dismiss behavior from men that does not align with how her world is constructed, in addition to her desires. Emotional maturity, meaning your ability to quickly deduce which behavior is postured to your world, and behavior that is not congruent with your desired outcomes, allows you to perpetually be available to the right type of man. This is so because no other man can waste her time and occupy her emotions.

Emotionally mature women have an eye to decipher silly and immature behavior in men and can recognize actions that are congruent with how she moves and sees the world. She is only compatible with the emotionally intelligent and mature man. She is postured only to him. This is how she does not get intertwined with men who could rob her of experiencing the quintessential black man.

The emotionally intelligent woman will not allow her emotions to override her logic and reason.

Consequently, she is rarely in compromising and undesirable positions. Her world is balanced and whole. The successful black man reveres her space, as it aligns with everything he embodies.

If you process information through intelligence gained from your experiences and the world around you, and operate with logic and reason, the successful black man will desire to share a space with you. The successful black man, who has constructed a life in his exact desired fashion, does not want to contend with the headaches of dealing with a woman who regularly engages in unintelligent behavior.

If you adhere to, internalize, and embrace the information in this book, you will be primed to attract the type of successful black man that you can build a healthy life with. I love you, black woman. There are many successful and whole black men who are waiting to encounter you. The mythical black man, who will acknowledge your value, cherish, revere, and respect you, while showing up as the best version of himself, does exist. You two will place one foot in front of the next and make to the Promised Land that awaits you two.

The Standard

I presented very applicable information, mindsets, and strategies to elevate your mind, body, and emotions; but you should always acknowledge and seek your Creator for wholeness, guidance, and revelation for your life. You will evolve into and become the woman any whole man will covet. Forget the statistics, your match exists. You two will find one another. Your preparedness for him will dictate the power and outcome of this encounter.

I celebrate you, black woman. You are cut from an unparalleled cloth. There is nothing that exists like you on the planet. As you undertake the continuous task of evolving into the best version of yourself, always understand there is a place where you end, and where God begins. You can empower yourself, but remember to pray to the All-Knowing Omniscient Creator for guidance.

Notes and Insights

Notes and Insights

Bonus Chapter:

Attraction

How To Be Appealing To Successful Black Men... For Black Women

Many women choose to focus on the lopsided statistics that exists with the ratio of successful black men to successful black women. With this reality, many women tend to settle for men who do not check important boxes that represent desirability for the man they'd like to partner with.

I'm here to express that you would rather go without than to get with a man just because society says there's a shortage of good black men. If you do not desire the man you are partnered with, you will always be susceptible and vulnerable to the man that you desire.

I believe marriage should be a one-time, all encompassing deal. I believe you should desire the person across from you to a degree that any person who crosses your path is irrelevant; regardless of how attractive they are, because your heart, energy, and essence are fixated on your spouse.

Desirability comes in many forms. I believe physical desirability to be one of the greatest in terms of importance. You should literally feel butterflies when you see your significant other due to how they are packaged existing in a boundless realm of fulfillment and appeal. You should have lust in your eyes for your spouse, because you will regularly encounter the man that you have that level of desire for.

Don't partner with the provider who checks important boxes, but not the category that will keep you interested, engaged, and bound to him.

Accept that it is okay to encounter men who have it all together who just don't do it for you. Deducing that you could be attracted to someone deeply as you two progress in years is important, and vital to the spice of your relationship.

The Reality of Desirability

When a man asks a woman to be his wife, he usually has concluded that no other woman can be adorned in packaging as complete and appealing as hers. She's captivated him on all levels, and his lifetime devotion to her is the evidence of this. He could have continued his pursuit of other women, but concluded that task would be meaningless, as everything he's ever hoped for is staring back at him in the form of the woman who he desires to be his wife.

She checks many boxes that are outside of his endless physical attraction to her, but we must acknowledge that he has a level of physical attraction to her that equates to him being satisfied with her as the only romantic interest for the rest of his life.

I've witnessed women accept that marriage proposal, understanding that man checks many important boxes that would solidify her long term wellbeing, but the important box of attraction is unchecked.

She is not fully into him, and he is into her so deeply that its depth cannot be quantified. These two individuals tie the knot, she hangs in there as long as she can, with her quality of life increasing as a result of his presence in her life, but the desirability just isn't there. She says things like, "Sometimes, I'm just not into my husband." Time progresses and she realizes the big house, nice car, and elevated lifestyle just doesn't do it for her. She departs. He didn't do anything but love and cherish her. He is devastated.

Range of Desirability

Some men just do it for you, and they're not the prototypical man you'd find attractive. This is where the range of desirability must be taken into the equation. It's not always about looks. It could be the man's confidence that captivates you, his drive, sense of humor, or personality that wins you over. Just make sure that whatever the quality is it captivates you and focuses your desire and attention completely on him if you are going to consider him for a lifetime.

The ideal packaging will cross your path. If you are not totally immersed in the man across from you, don't do it. You are on borrowed time.

I see married women all the time who are wed to great men that they don't desire in totality. They don't have to say a word, but you can easily pick up on their available energy when in the presence of the man they lust for. These are the women who go out there and explore, and then feel devastated because they have a conscience; or they feel liberated because a piece of themselves they knew was incomplete, has now been gratified.

You don't have to venture out, only to return devastated to the good man in your life you truly don't desire. If he checks all of the boxes minus the glaring category of desirability, deem him as not for you.

It is better to go without, then to contend with the reality of sharing a space with a man you are not completely into.

You Know

You know the man that you desire. Even if it is not one fixating characteristic, you know this man when you encounter him. Given that your lens is clear on the type of man that does it for you, become a match for this man. Be the absolute best version of yourself so that this man, who completely does it for you, won't escape your grasp.

You are in control of how you show up to this man. He possesses the characteristics I consistently reiterated in this book, but he is tailored to your fashion. You know this man when you see him. Be packaged in a way that is undeniable. Be in your best physical condition and maintain your best appearance so he knows this is a lifestyle for you, and not a trend.

We must make no apologies when it comes to what does it for us in an ideal significant other. Fulfillment comes when the boxes we desire are checked. Ask yourself the important question: Does the man who fancies me give me the sensation that I could be satisfied with just him for a lifetime? Your answer will allow you to see around corners.

Anchored

You can be connected to or anchored to the man you are with. When a woman is connected to her man she can meet a man that she is extremely attracted to and have to pull herself back from the situation because she has a level of attraction to this man in her space that she doesn't to her man. She will visibly display that she needs to go before she makes a decision she regrets. She does the right thing, which is respectable, but she has to force her way out the energy field of the man that she is really attracted to.

How To Be Appealing To Successful Black Men... For Black Women

A woman meets a man that she finds very attractive. She concludes that this is a nice-looking guy, but she has no available energy for this guy, and the man at home completely does it for her. She is not available to this attractive man she just met because she is so fulfilled with and attracted to the man at home that she is anchored to him.

I meet women all the time that I find attractive. Sometimes I'll just be talking to a woman, and I'll shift the conversation and say, "You have a man, don't you?" She'll say, "How did you know?" I respond with, "Because I felt his energy on you."

This happened because she was present with me in the moment we met, and I could deduce she may have found me attractive. But in reality, she was in no way available to me because she was fulfilled and anchored to the one that she was encapsulated with.

Select the man who you can sink your anchor into and experience the type of experience and attraction that involuntarily intensifies, and that exists outside of time and space.

Notes and Insights

Notes and Insights

About The Author

How To Be Appealing To Successful Black Men... For Black Women

Matthew C. Horne, motivational speaker and author, is the president of Optimum Success International, a speaking and publishing company located in the metropolitan Washington, DC area. He is an international authority on Maximizing Human Potential. Matthew is the author of *The Universe Is Inviting You In,* and *All We Have Is NOW,* which are both publicly endorsed by legendary motivational speaker Les Brown. He is also the author of *Choices: The Young Black Man's Guide to Successful Living, How to Get Beautiful Women ...and Everything Else You Want From Life, The Successful Dreamer,* and *How To Be Appealing To Successful Black Men ...For Black Women.* Growing up, Matthew's ultimate vision for his life was to play basketball in the NBA. He positioned himself to live this reality through obtaining a full-athletic scholarship to play Division I basketball in college. Much to his surprise destiny revealed his true calling during his collegiate years, as he discovered a passion for motivational speaking. Matthew was told by his professors he would never make it as an English major, and to the astonishment of everyone, he not only obtained a Bachelor of Arts Degree in English, but also was offered his first book contract before he graduated in his last semester of college. Matthew's message is one of creating your own reality according to your vivid destiny pictures. Matthew empowers audiences to live their unique truth, independent of the opinions of others. Matthew is also developing a voice in the relationship and dating world through his literary offerings and media appearances. Matthew's message is quickly spanning the globe through his books, audios, and motivational speeches. He has served as a guest-columnist for the *Washington Post's* "The Root DC" section. He is the creator of the television show "Matthew C. Horne Live!" He has also been featured on the legendary radio station WOL with his weekly minute motivational segments. Matthew also owns Lightning Fast Book Publishing, a company that publishes author's books in three weeks. Matthew C. Horne also owns Matthew C. Horne Author PR, Marketing, and Management, a company that provides a full range of public relations services for authors of any genre. Matthew is available for speeches, radio and television interviews, and book signings. All who encounter Matthew C. Horne, will leave with a heightened awareness of their limitless possibilities, and be positioned to live their Best Life Possible. To learn more about Matthew C. Horne, please visit www.matthewchorne.com.

Matthew C. Horne's Additional Titles

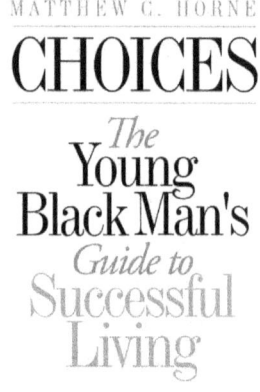

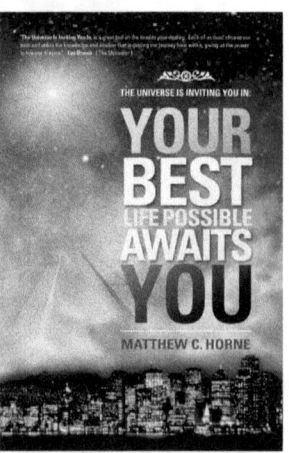

Available at: www.matthewchorne.com

Services

Motivational Speaking/Book Publishing/Public Relations for Authors

Motivational Speaking: Matthew C. Horne is the world's premier motivational speaker and leading authority in Maximizing Human Potential. His message has spanned the globe and will bring any audience to life through an awareness of their limitless possibilities and creative potential. Matthew is available for speeches, lectures, seminars, radio, and television interviews.

Testimonial:

Thank you very much for your recent motivational speech on "Peak Performance in the Workplace." I am very appreciative of what you delivered to our employees here at NASA Goddard Space Flight Center.

You brought your experience to the table and stressed teamwork. Your entire presentation was value-added. In a brief period of time, you stressed how employees can achieve peak performance by valuing their work and bringing their best work and attitude to everything they attempt.

—**Michael P. Kelly**
Chief, Institutional Support Office, NASA Goddard Space Flight Center

Book Publishing

Matthew C. Horne's book publishing company, *Lightning Fast Book Publishing* is a full service book publishing company, which produces books, and builds the author's overall platform to become a reputable public figure. Matthew's company has a personal touch, as he is heavily involved in the production of every author's book, and implements the same strategies for book production and distribution that are responsible for Matthew's decade plus long career as a successful globally selling author. Services range from book editing, cover design to website design and global sales and distribution for author's books. To learn more about *Lightning Fast Book Publishing* please visit www.lfbookpublishing.com.

> **Testimonial:** The Lightning Fast Book Publishing Team over delivered in their publishing of my book, "G.R.A.C.E: God's Reconstruction After Cancer Exits." My fully designed, edited, and printed book was finished in two-and a-half weeks. The symbolism on the book cover captured my books' content in totality. Lightning Fast Book Publishing is the premier company for all of your book publishing needs!
>
> **Bonnie Crittendon-Powell, Author of "Grace: God's Reconstruction After Cancer Exits"**

Public Relations for Authors

Matthew C. Horne Author PR, Marketing and Management is a Public Relations company that specializes exclusively in promoting authors. Every author receives a tailored Public Relations strategy to get each author to his or her desired outcome as an author. Matthew's experience with having publicists in the past has been all excuses and no results. Matthew C. Horne served as his own PR, Marketing, and Management team throughout the years, culminating into a very successful career entrenched in longevity. Matthew C. Horne recreates this experience for every author he represents. For more information, please visit www.matthewchorneauthorpr.com.

Testimonial: When it came to marketing my novels, there were those who promised me the world, but it was Matthew C. Horne Author PR, Marketing and Management that actually brought the dream to reality. This company coached me with excellent strategies for selling, put me in touch with outstanding entrepreneurs, increased my book signing events tremendously, and supplied engagements on both radio and internet shows where I gained world-wide exposure. Today, I can honestly say that I am selling far more books than ever before, and, with the help of this company, I am in touch with a community of business people who continue to connect with me in a multiplicity of ways. Matthew C. Horne commandeers a superb company that guarantees excellence and makes no excuse for anything less.

Doris H. Dancy, Author
The Redemptive Love Series:
Jagged Edges
Shattered Pieces
All Other Ground

www.ingramcontent.com/pod-product-compliance
Lightning Source LLC
Chambersburg PA
CBHW050350230426
43663CB00010B/2066